STEP-BY-STEP # knitting

A COMPLETE INTRODUCTION TO THE CRAFT OF KNITTING

INCLUDING PHOTOGRAPHS IN FULL COLOR

by Mary Walker Phillips

DESIGNED BY AND PRODUCED UNDER

THE SUPERVISION OF WILLIAM AND SHIRLEY SAYLES

GOLDEN PRESS · NEW YORK

Foreword

Of all fabrics knits are, to me, some of the most wonderful. Knitting, by nature, is resilient and pliable, conforming to the shape of the body. The open construction breathes; the airy loft of knitted cloth is warm and cosy. As I work on complex, costly weaving apparatus, I have long envied the simplicity and directness of knitting. I also envy the silence and portability.

Partly because of a new freedom in yarn selection and partly because of the rediscovery of texture and color potentials, knitting today is in its most creative phase in hundreds of years. Because knitting is ideally suited to automated production of finished products, machine knitting will probably usurp much of the market that woven goods now have. This revolution will be hastened and humanized by the creative, open-ended attitude of today's handknitter.

Mary Walker Phillips is ideally suited to lead this revolution. As the reader will soon see, she combines inspiration with taste and common sense, energy with organization. She is the great knitter of our time. She has taken knitting out of the socks-and-sweater doldrums to prove that knit fabric can be a blanket, a pillow, a piece of art. In this book she illustrates the fact that people in other cultures have often done this. Perhaps more importantly she demonstrates that knitting is a creative medium of self expression.

I hope that she has many disciples of the sort that will not only do what she does, but follow her lead in doing what has not been done. I hope that some leaders, having mastered the simple techniques and gained insight into the broad range of potentials, will strike out into new areas. Can rope be knit? Can wire? Can a hammock? Can a piece of sculpture? Of course! Read on.

Jack Lenor Larsen, Designer

President of Jack Lenor Larsen, Inc.

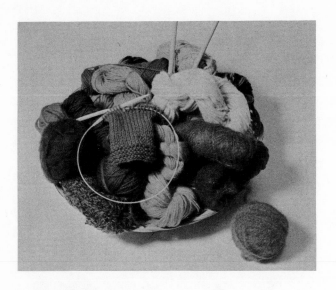

contents

acknowledgments

Thanks are due to the Alliance for Progress and to the
Brooklyn Museum for permission to photograph
items from their collections. Thanks also go to Mr. and
Mrs. Bob Carr and Mr. and Mrs. Anthony Saris
who so graciously allowed their homes to be used as
background for many of the photographs shown here.
Among those who have assisted in the preparation
of this book, special thanks are due to:

Robin Greene, *Assistant Editor*
Hal Halverstadt, *Consultant*
Betty MacDonald, *Design*
Louis Mervar, *Photography*
Catherine Scholtz, *Artist*

introduction

Knitting is a stimulating craft,—it can be learned quickly, the materials and equipment used are inexpensive and easy to store, and you can take your knitting with you wherever you go. You will be surprised at how soon a project can be completed when knitting is done at odd moments—while visiting with friends, attending a meeting, riding in a car or bus.

Today with so many types and colors of yarn available and with the influence that fashion has had upon the design of knitted items, hand-knitting is probably more widely popular than ever before in its entire history.

There was a golden age of knitting during the Tudor and Elizabethan periods and, at that time, men were apprenticed to Guilds for six years to become master knitters. A man would spend the first three of those years learning the fundamentals of knitting and the next three abroad studying techniques of other countries. At the end of this period, he was given thirteen weeks in which to complete a woolen shirt, a pair of woolen socks with clocks, and a carpet of intricate design which had to be absolutely original. These items were submitted to examination by the Guild for acceptance before the apprentice could become a full member.

The decline of hand knitting also came during this era. The Reverend William Lee invented a frame knitting machine and around this simple device was developed the machine-knit hosiery industry; first in England and then in other parts of the world.

It is generally believed that knitting started well before Christianity among the nomadic people of the Arabian Desert, that it then spread to Egypt and from there to Spain and the rest of Europe. Arabic color knitting has played an important part in the evolution of knitting and fine examples of it have been found in Egypt. (The elaborate pattern of fine crossed

Bolivian wool cap with ear flaps, typical wear of villagers in the mountain areas. A fine example of color design. Brooklyn Museum.

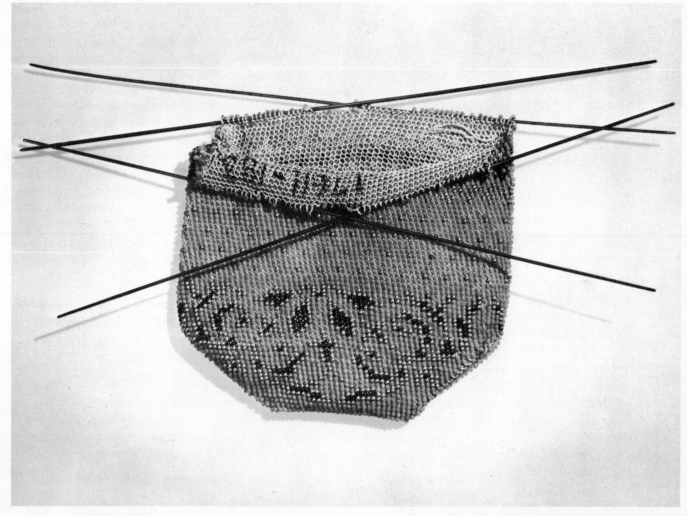

Purse knit with four needles. The beads are threaded according to a carefully planned design so that they come at the correct point in the fabric. Margaret Bedell Collection, Brooklyn Museum.

Eastern stitch is 36 stitches to the inch.) One of the earliest knitted fabrics unearthed is a pair of woolen sandal socks of plain stockinette stitch, probably made on a circular frame.

The peak of Spanish and Florentine knitting was reached in the twelfth through fourteenth centuries, and the work done then shows the influence of the Arabic color knitting. In France knitting was concentrated mainly on hosiery, while Germany and Austria became known for their heavily-cabled natural wool fabrics, on which colorful patterns were often embroidered.

In this book there are photographs which show knitting examples of the past, the present, and of other countries. Some of these photographs were selected for their exciting use of color and others to give some idea of the wide range of creative possibilities in this craft.

The projects offered in this book were designed and executed by the author. They are worked in simple stitches as well as in more intricate ones, and at least one easy project is included with every selection.

Nothing in this book requires fittings—everything

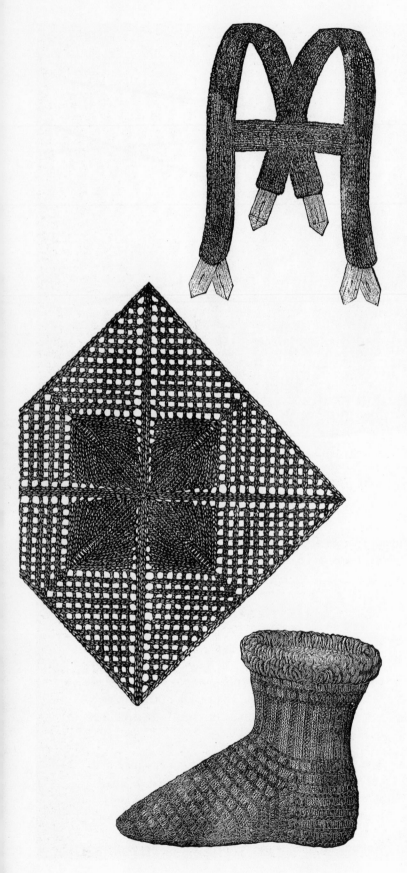

is straight knitting. When you don't have to be concerned with the fit of a garment, there is more freedom for experimentation. And by knitting items for the home, a wider variety of possible projects is available to you.

The items presented include various scarves, stoles, and blankets, rugs, and a stair runner, reversible sofa pillows, floor pillows, a Greek-style purse, and lace-like placemats that when starched resemble raffia. The knitting instructions are step-by-step and clearly diagrammed. Every project is shown in color and in close-up detail. There are hints to help you improve your knitting, descriptions of popular pattern stitches and some useful information so that you will be encouraged to make your own designs.

At the conclusion of this book there is a list of suppliers for yarns and equipment and one for books and periodicals. There is also a foreign language key to the knitting abbreviations.

I hope that all knitters—the more experienced as well as the beginner—will be stimulated by the selections in this book. And I also hope that you will gain enough inspiration and confidence to go on to create your own designs and projects.

Good luck and good knitting.

(Left) Three examples of early American knitting: pair of boy's braces; knitting pattern for a counterpane or bed spread; and a knitted sleeping sock.

Wall hanging, "Lace Diadem," designed and knit by the author. Knitting as an art form is a contemporary innovation and one that you might find challenging.

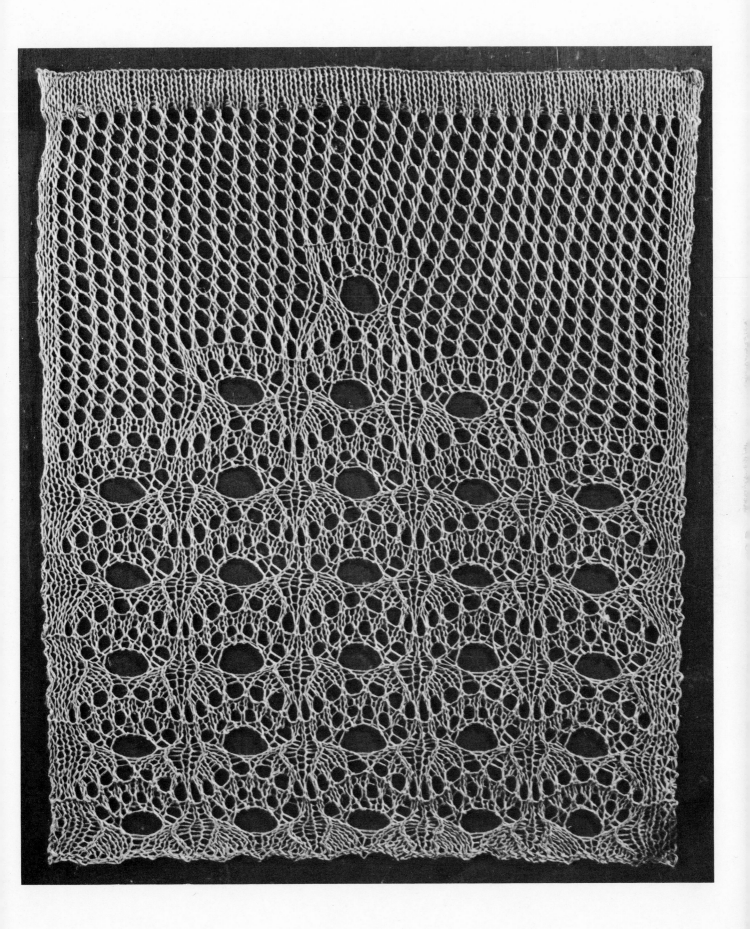

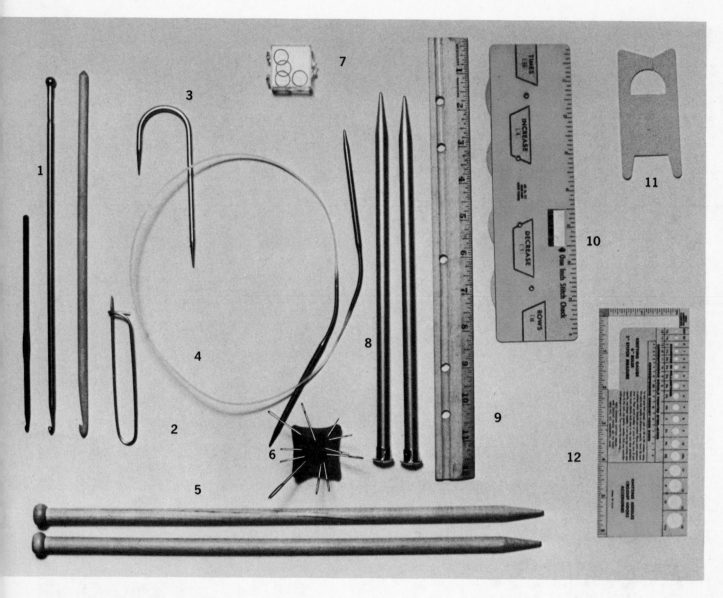

equipment

Knitting equipment not shown here includes: double pointed needles (p. 33), needle point guards (to prevent stitches from sliding off needle when work is set aside), tapestry needles, rustproof "T" pins, and scissors. You may, if you wish, make your own knitting needles from dowels. New aids for the knitter constantly appear on the market, and you will always be tempted to add to your supply.

1. crochet hooks (metal & wooden)
2. stitch holder
3. cable stitch holder
4. circular knitting needle (see p. 33)
5. wooden knitting needles
6. pin cushion
7. markers (see p. 33)
8. metal knitting needles
9. ruler
10. stitch and row counter
11. bobbin
12. needle gauge and gauge check

abbreviated knitting terms

K	knit
P	purl
ST(S)	stitch(es)
YO	yarn over [needle]
SL	slip [stitch]†
TOG	together
PSSO	pass slip stitch over [next stitch]
DP	double pointed (needles)
INC	increase
DEC	decrease

†always slip stitch as if to purl unless otherwise directed.

abbreviated crochet terms

CH	chain
SC	single crochet
*****	asterisk—work the directions from the * as many times as directed

yarns

A wide variety of materials are suitable for knitting, including wool, cotton, linen, silk, synthetic fibers, metallic yarns, string, straw, or anything else you may discover.

Today's yarns are usually colorfast, but you may wish to test your yarn by washing a section of it before beginning to knit.

It is difficult to know exactly how much yarn a particular project will require. Usually knitting yarns are sold by weight, and the amount of yarn in a skein or ball will vary according to the type of yarn and the brand. To get some idea of the quantity of yarn you will require, refer to other instructions that require a similar yarn for a similar item. After using one skein or ball of your yarn, measure how much fabric you have completed. Will you need more yarn or do you have enough?

Always buy more yarn than you think you will need; in this way you will be sure of having all your skeins of the same dye lot. Unopened balls and skeins can usually be returned within a reasonable length of time after purchase. However, smaller amounts of yarn need not be wasted; in some of the projects given they are used in amounts ranging from half

an ounce upward. Wash used yarn to remove kinks before knitting with it again.

Specific colors are asked for in the projects but since yarn companies discontinue some colors and introduce others, substitute where necessary.

ball winding

Yarn must be wound very loosely to prevent it from becoming stretched. Wind the yarn over your fingers as shown, then slip the yarn onto the ball.

casting on

Right Hand

METHOD 1

Never cast on too tightly. To begin casting on, make a slip knot at a distance from the end of the yarn strand. To determine the length of this "free end" yarn, plan for about 1″ of yarn per stitch for heavy rug yarn and large needles and ½″ of yarn per stitch for light-weight yarn and small needles. You cast on by working the free end in with the ball yarn.

FIGS. 1 & 2 Make a slip knot, place loop on needle and tighten.

Fig. 1

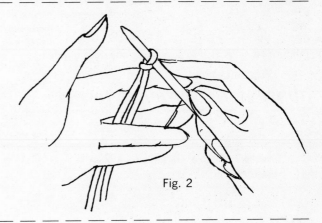

Fig. 2

FIG. 3 With needle in right hand, insert left thumb under free end yarn. The yarn that is attached to the ball goes over the left forefinger. Hold this yarn taut by slipping it under the middle finger of the left hand.

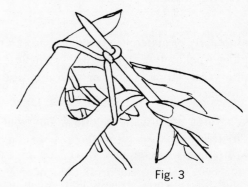

Fig. 3

FIGS. 4-6 With left thumb, pull free end yarn out to form loop. Insert needle into this loop and draw yarn through loop, forming new stitch. *with thread on ball being under + over needle.*

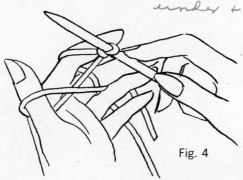

Fig. 4

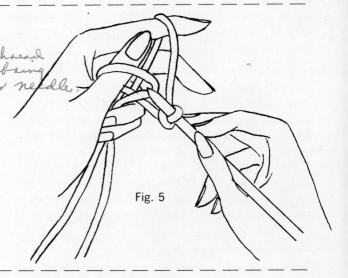

Fig. 5

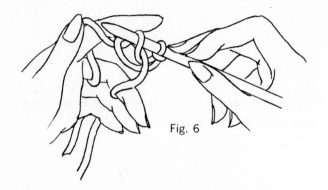

Fig. 6

FIG. 7. With left thumb, pull free end yarn to bring new stitch close to needle. Repeat directions for Figs. 3–7 for required number of stitches.

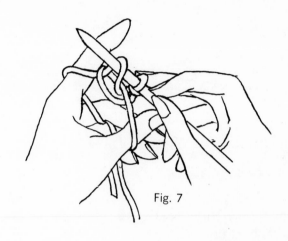

Fig. 7

METHOD 2

Never cast on too tightly. This method of casting on uses the Knit stitch.

Make a slip knot, place it on needle and tighten. (See Fig. 1 in Method 1.)

FIG. 1 & 2 Hold needle in left hand, insert right needle into front side of stitch, front to back; bring yarn under and over right needle point. Draw yarn through stitch, forming new stitch. Keep stitch on right needle.

FIG. 3 Insert left needle into front side of stitch, front to back, and slip stitch off right needle. Repeat directions for Figs. 1–3 for required number of stitches.

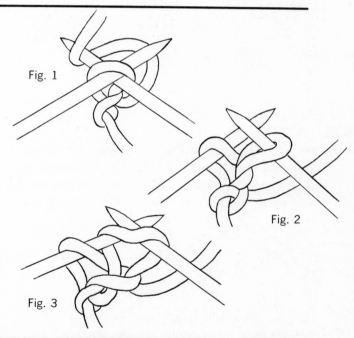

Fig. 1

Fig. 2

Fig. 3

selvedge treatment

When knitting first row after casting on, insert right needle into *front* side of stitch (Fig. 4) for an edge with a lot of stretch, good for such items as hats. If you wish a firmer edge with minimal stretch, as for rugs, insert needle into *back* side of stitch (Fig. 5). This principle applies to knitting as well as to casting on. For a firmer fabric, knit and purl into the *back* side of the stitches.

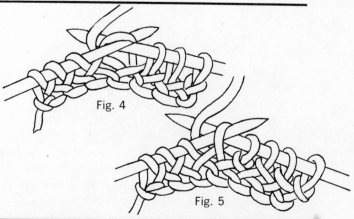

Fig. 4

Fig. 5

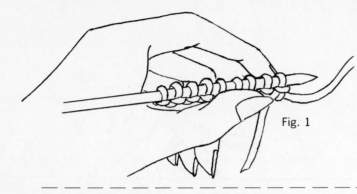

Fig. 1

how to knit

Right Hand

FIG. 1 Hold needle with stitches in left hand. Keep yarn at back of work.

FIG. 2 Insert right needle into front side of first stitch, front to back.

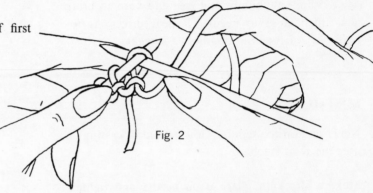

Fig. 2

Fig. 4

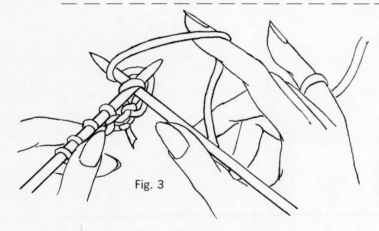

Fig. 3

FIGS. 3 & 4 Bring yarn under and over right needle point and draw yarn through stitch, forming new stitch.

FIG. 5 Keep new stitch on right needle and slip old stitch off left needle. Repeat directions for Figs. 2–5 for required number of stitches.

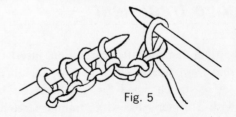

Fig. 5

NOTE: Be sure to keep each stitch to be worked near the tip of the left needle so it can be drawn off needle easily when knit.

how to purl

Right Hand

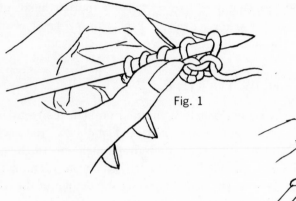

Fig. 1

FIGS. 1 & 2 Keep yarn at front of work. Insert right needle into front side of stitch, back to front.

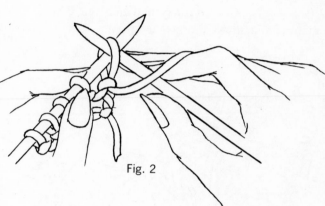

Fig. 2

FIG. 3 Bring yarn over and under right needle point.

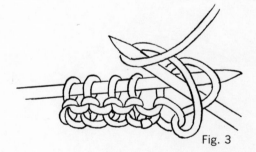

Fig. 3

FIGS. 4-6 Draw yarn through stitch, forming new stitch. Slip off left needle. Repeat directions for Figs. 2-6 for required number of stitches.

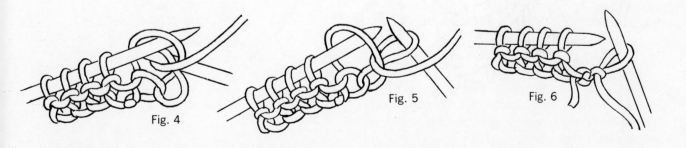

Fig. 4

Fig. 5

Fig. 6

---

continental method of knitting

Right Hand

There is a great advantage in knowing two methods of holding the yarn when knitting. It is very useful for knitting with two or more colors on the same row (see p. 27). Also, you may find that the Continental method allows you greater speed.

The strand of yarn is held in the left hand, over the forefinger, and is kept taut by being woven around the other fingers of the left hand.

HOW TO KNIT

The right needle is inserted through the front side of the stitch, front to back. The point of the needle catches the yarn, pulls it through the stitch, and slips the stitch off the left needle in a continuous motion. The arrow indicates the motion of the right needle in catching the yarn.

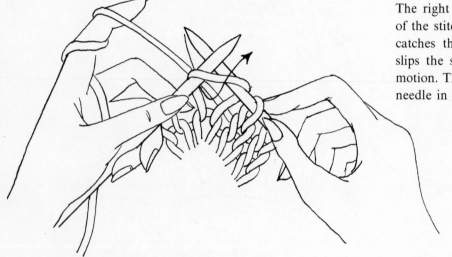

HOW TO PURL

The right needle is inserted through the front side of the stitch, back to front. The point of the needle catches the yarn, pulls it through the stitch, and slips the stitch off the left needle in a continuous motion. The arrow indicates the motion of the right needle in catching the yarn.

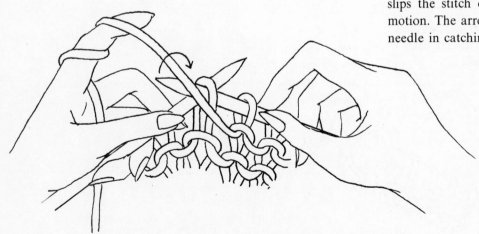

how to increase

Right Hand

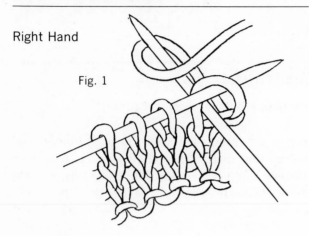

Fig. 1

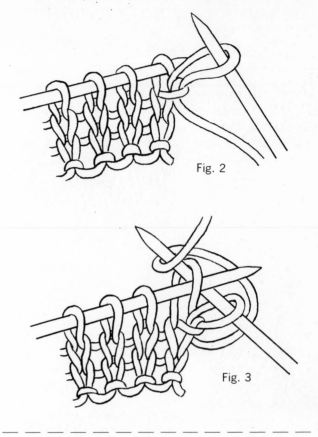

Fig. 2

Fig. 3

METHOD 1

Knitting Twice into Same Stitch

FIGS. 1 & 2 Knit a stitch, leaving it on left needle.
FIG. 3 Knit the same stitch again, this time knitting into *back* side of stitch, forming second new stitch. Slip off left needle.

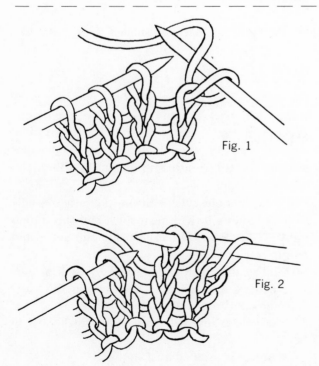

Fig. 1

Fig. 2

METHOD 2

Yarn Over (YO)

FIG. 1 Knit a stitch. Loop yarn around right needle, under and over, forming new stitch.
FIG. 2 Knit next stitch.
NOTE: Method 2, the YO stitch, is used in lace stitches (see p. 29). When no hole is desired in the fabric, work into *back* of YO on next row.

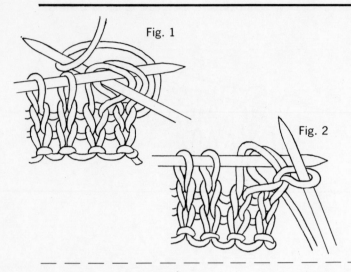

Fig. 1

Fig. 2

how to decrease

Right Hand

METHOD 1

Knitting 2 Stitches Together (front)

FIGS. 1 & 2 Insert right needle through front side of second and first stitches, front to back. Knit both stitches together and slip off left needle. On the fabric the decrease stitches slant to the right.

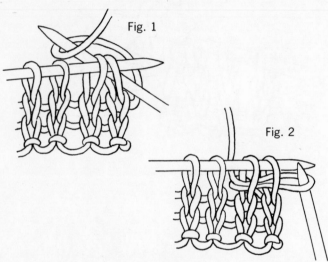

Fig. 1

Fig. 2

METHOD 2

Knitting 2 Stitches Together (back)

FIGS. 1 & 2 Insert right needle through *back* side of first and second stitches, knit both stitches together, and slip off left needle.

On the fabric the decrease stitches slant to the left.

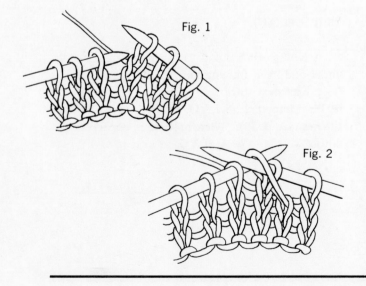

Fig. 1

Fig. 2

METHOD 3

Passing Slip Stitch over Knit Stitch (PSSO)

FIGS. 1 & 2 Slip one stitch knitwise* onto right needle without knitting it. Knit next stitch and slip it onto right needle. Insert left needle into slip stitch and pull it over the knit stitch.

NOTE: The slip stitch can be used by itself as part of a pattern, and not as a decrease. In this case, slip stitch purlwise† unless otherwise directed.

*The needle is inserted through the stitch as if to knit.

†The needle is inserted as if to purl.

binding off

Right Hand

FIGS 1-4 Knit 2 stitches. Insert left needle into second stitch on right needle and pull it over the first stitch. Repeat directions until 1 stitch remains. Pull first stitch over second and draw yarn through remaining stitch. Cut yarn, leaving an end of 2 or 3 inches to be woven into fabric with tapestry needle or crochet hook.

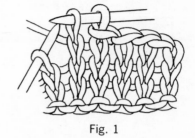

Fig. 1

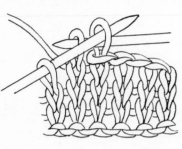

Fig. 2

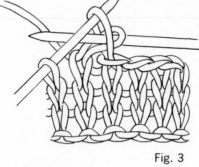

Fig. 3

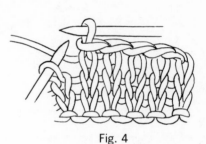

Fig. 4

NOTE: You should usually bind off *in pattern* unless otherwise directed.

gauge

The Golden Rule of Knitting

Gauge is the number of stitches per inch and the number of rows per inch. Knitting directions give gauge information that must be followed to insure that the item will be the specified size. *It is imperative that you check your gauge before beginning a project.* Make a sample of knitting of at least 2 pattern repeats, or approximately 4 inches square. Block this sample and measure a 2 inch square section to check your gauge. To make stitches tighter, use needles one size smaller; to make stitches looser use one size larger. If you are having trouble getting your row gauge correct, it is sometimes helpful to use a needle one size larger or smaller on *purl* rows.

NOTE: The gauges specified in this book apply *after blocking*.

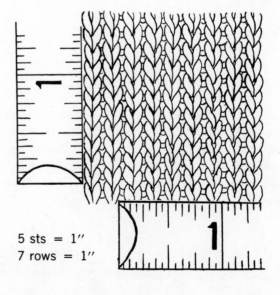

5 sts = 1″
7 rows = 1″

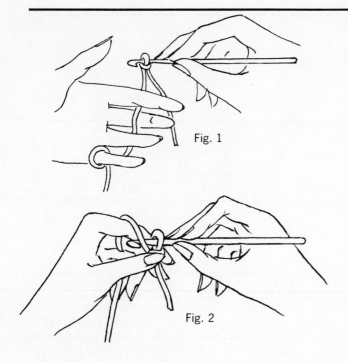

Fig. 1

Fig. 2

how to crochet

Right Hand

FIGS. 1 & 2 Make a slip knot near end of yarn, leaving a short end. With crochet hook in right hand, held as you would hold a pencil, insert hook through slip knot stitch and tighten stitch on hook. Yarn is kept in the left hand, looped over forefinger and wrapped around little finger to adjust tension. The free end is held at base of stitch by thumb and forefinger.

CHAIN STITCH

FIGS. 3 & 4 Insert hook through slip knot stitch and under yarn strand on forefinger. Pull strand through stitch, making one chain stitch. Repeat directions for required number of chain stitches.

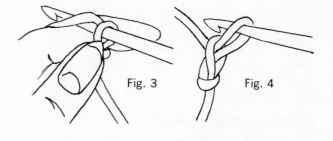

Fig. 3   Fig. 4

SINGLE CROCHET STITCH

FIG. 5 The single crochet is worked on a foundation row of chain stitches, as are all crochet stitches. Leave last chain completed on hook. Insert hook, front to back, under two top loops of second chain stitch from end, and under yarn strand. Pull yarn through loops, leaving two stitches on hook.

FIG. 6 Insert hook under yarn strand and pull through both stitches, leaving one stitch on hook.

Insert hook under two top loops of next chain stitch, and repeat directions. After last single crochet stitch of each row has been worked, chain one stitch before starting next row. On next and all following rows, begin single crochet stitch in *first* stitch on row below.

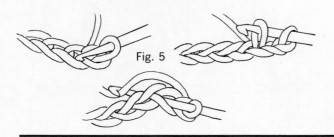

Fig. 5

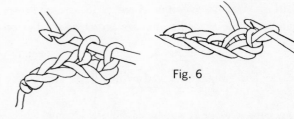

Fig. 6

fringe

Wrap yarn around length of 12-inch ruler and cut at both ends.

FIG. 1 Fold desired number of strands in half.
FIGS. 2–5 With right side of fabric facing, draw strands through to back side with crochet hook, pull ends through loop and tighten.

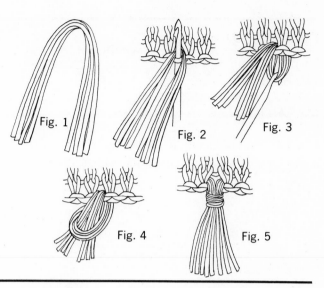

Fig. 1

Fig. 2

Fig. 3

Fig. 4

Fig. 5

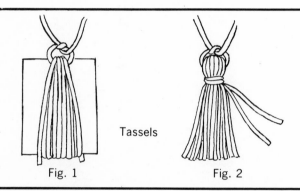

Tassels

Fig. 1

Fig. 2

tassels

FIG. 1 Wrap yarn around cardboard of desired size. Tie a piece of yarn around the strands at the top.
FIG. 2 Cut strands at bottom and tie another piece of yarn around strands about one-third of the way down. Attach to knitting by tying with aid of hook or needle.

blocking

Before blocking your knitting, mark off correct measurements by the inch on a piece of brown paper or sheet. Place under knitting when you block.

Immerse knitting in warm water, but do not soak. Remove from water and gently press out excess water, *do not wring*. Roll knitting between two towels to remove as much moisture as possible. Place knitting on flat surface and adjust to proper measurements. Pin around all sides every inch or closer, using heavy rustproof "T" pins, or heavy straight pins. Be careful to keep edges straight. Do not dry in the sun or next to a radiator.

NOTE: Blankets and stoles should be folded before being immersed in water to render easier handling when wet. Fabric softener should be added to the rinse water for these two items.

If an item is to be sewn, block before sewing.

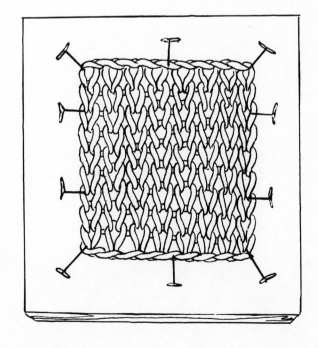

casting on

Left Hand

METHOD 1

Never cast on too tightly. To begin casting on, make a slip knot at a distance from the end of the yarn strand. To determine the length of this "free end" yarn, plan for about 1″ of yarn per stitch for heavy rug yarn and large needles, and ½″ of yarn per stitch for lightweight yarn and small needles. You cast on by working the free end in with the ball yarn.

FIGS. 1 & 2 Make a slip knot, place loop on needle and tighten.

Fig. 1

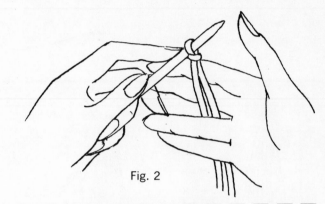

Fig. 2

FIG. 3 With needle in left hand, insert right thumb under free end yarn. The yarn that is attached to the ball goes over the right forefinger. Hold this yarn taut by slipping it under the middle finger of the right hand.

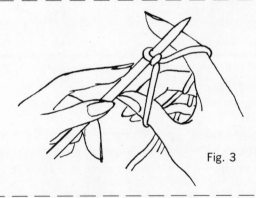

Fig. 3

FIGS. 4-6 With right thumb, pull free end yarn out to form loop. Insert needle into this loop and draw yarn through loop, forming new stitch.

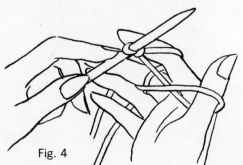

Fig. 4

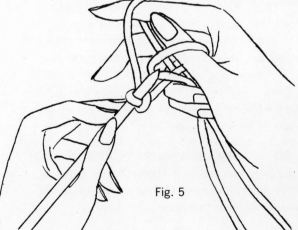

Fig. 5

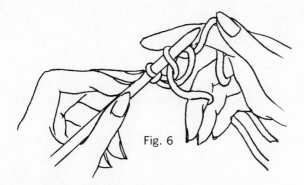

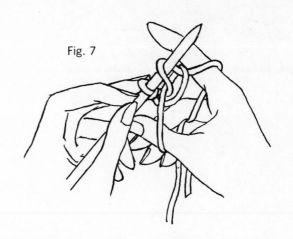

Fig. 7

FIG. 7 With right thumb, pull free end yarn to bring new stitch close to needle. Repeat directions for Figs. 3–7 for required number of stitches.

METHOD 2

Left Hand

Never cast on too tightly.

This method of casting on uses the Knit stitch.

Make a slip knot, place it on needle and tighten, as in Fig. 1, Method 1.

FIG. 1 Hold needle in right hand, insert left needle into front side of stitch, front to back; bring yarn under and over left needle point.

FIG. 2 Draw yarn through stitch, forming new stitch. Keep stitch on left needle.

FIG. 3 Insert right needle into front side of stitch, front to back, and slip stitch off left needle. Repeat directions for Figs. 1–3 for required number of stitches.

Fig. 1

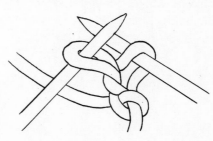

Fig. 2

selvedge treatment

When knitting first row after casting on, insert left needle into *front* side of stitch for an edge with a lot of stretch, good for such items as hats. If you wish a firmer edge with minimal stretch, as for rugs, insert needle into *back* side of stitch (Fig. 5). This principle applies to knitting as well as to casting on. For a firmer fabric, knit and purl into the *back* side of the stitches.

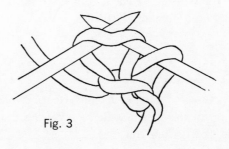

Fig. 3

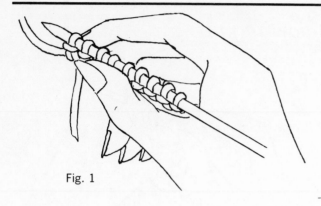

Fig. 1

how to knit

Left Hand

FIG. 1 Hold needle with stitches in right hand. Keep yarn at back of work.

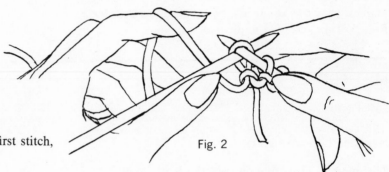

Fig. 2

FIG. 2 Insert left needle into front side of first stitch, front to back.

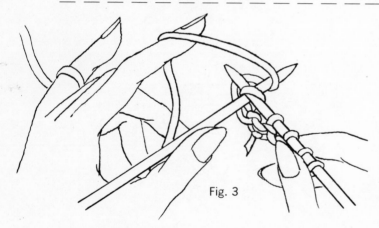

Fig. 3

Fig. 4

FIGS. 3 & 4 Bring yarn under and over left needle point and draw yarn through stitch, forming new stitch.

FIG. 5 Keep new stitch on left needle and slip old stitch off right needle. Repeat directions for Figs. 2–5 for required number of stitches.

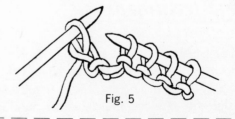

Fig. 5

NOTE: Be sure to keep each stitch to be worked near the tip of the right needle so it can be drawn off needle easily when knit.

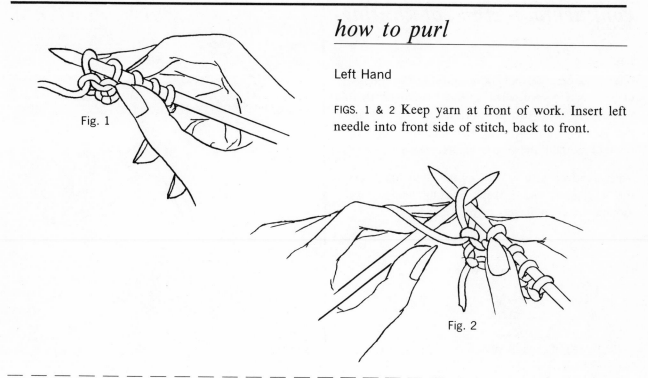

Fig. 1

how to purl

Left Hand

FIGS. 1 & 2 Keep yarn at front of work. Insert left needle into front side of stitch, back to front.

Fig. 2

FIG. 3 Bring yarn over and under left needle point.

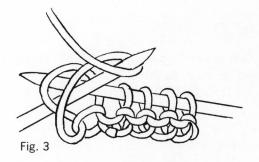

Fig. 3

FIGS. 4–6 Draw yarn through stitch, forming new stitch. Slip off right needle. Repeat directions for Figs. 2–6 for required number of stitches.

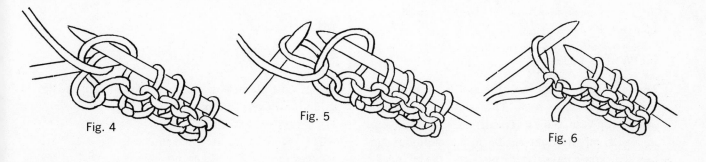

Fig. 4

Fig. 5

Fig. 6

continental method of knitting

Left Hand

There is a great advantage in knowing two methods of holding the yarn when knitting. It is very useful for knitting with two or more colors on the same row (see p. 27). Also, you may find that the Continental method allows you greater speed.

The strand of yarn is held in the right hand, over the forefinger, and is kept taut by being woven around the other fingers of the right hand.

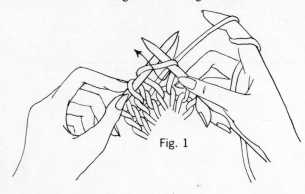

Fig. 1

HOW TO KNIT

The left needle is inserted through the front side of the stitch, back to front. The point of the needle catches the yarn, pulls it through the stitch and slips the stitch off the right needle in a continuous motion. The arrow indicates the motion of the left needle in catching the yarn.

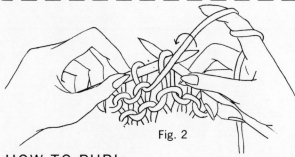

Fig. 2

HOW TO PURL

The left needle is inserted through the front side of the stitch, front to back. The point of the needle catches the yarn, pulls it through the stitch, and slips the stitch off the right needle in a continuous motion. The arrow indicates the motion of the left needle in catching the yarn.

how to increase

Left Hand

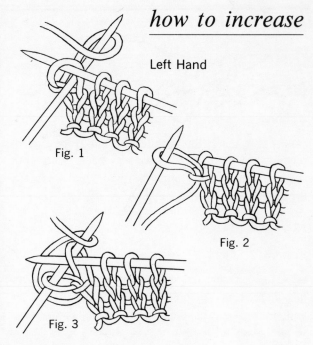

Fig. 1

Fig. 2

Fig. 3

METHOD 1

Knitting Twice into Same Stitch

FIGS. 1 & 2 Knit a stitch, leaving it on right needle. FIG. 3 Knit the same stitch again, this time knitting into *back* side of stitch, forming second new stitch. Slip off right needle.

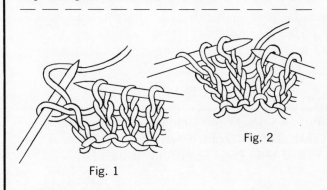

Fig. 1

Fig. 2

METHOD 2

Yarn Over (YO)

FIG. 1 Knit a stitch. Loop yarn around left needle, under and over, forming new stitch.
FIG. 2 Knit next stitch.
NOTE: Method 2, the YO stitch, is used in lace stitches (see p. 29). When no hole is desired in the fabric, work into *back* of YO stitch on next row.

how to decrease

Left Hand

METHOD 1

Knitting 2 Stitches Together (front)

FIGS. 1 & 2 Insert left needle through front side of second and first stitches, front to back. Knit both stitches together and slip off right needle. On the fabric the decrease stitches slant to the left.

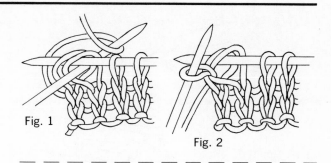

Fig. 1

Fig. 2

METHOD 2

Knitting 2 Stitches Together (back)

FIGS. 1 & 2 Insert left needle through *back* side of first and second stitches. Knit both stitches together and slip off right needle. On the fabric the decrease stitches slant to the left.

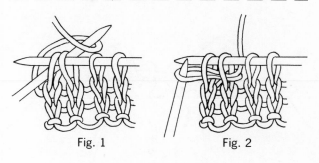

Fig. 1

Fig. 2

METHOD 3

Passing Slip Stitch Over Knit Stitch (PSSO)

FIGS. 1 & 2 Slip one stitch knitwise* onto left needle without knitting it. Knit next stitch and slip it onto left needle. Insert right needle into slip stitch and pull it over the knit stitch.

NOTE: The slip stitch can be used by itself as part of a pattern, and not as a decrease. In this case, slip stitch purlwise† unless otherwise directed.

*The needle is inserted through the stitch as if to knit.

†The needle is inserted as if to purl.

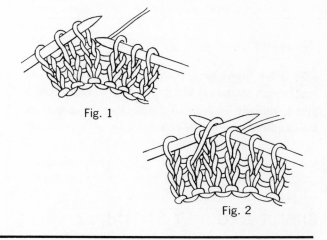

Fig. 1

Fig. 2

binding off

Left Hand

FIGS. 1-4 Knit 2 stitches. Insert right needle into second stitch on left needle and pull it over the first stitch. Repeat directions until 1 stitch remains. Pull first stitch over second and draw yarn through remaining stitch. Cut yarn, leaving an end of 2 or 3 inches to be woven into fabric with tapestry needle or crochet hook. For finishing see p. 19.

NOTE: You should usually bind off *in pattern* unless otherwise directed.

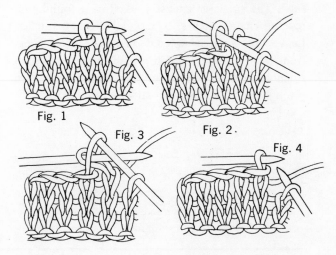

Fig. 1

Fig. 2

Fig. 3

Fig. 4

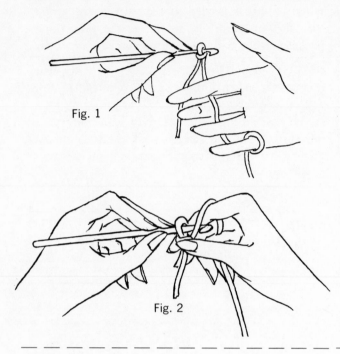

Fig. 1

Fig. 2

how to crochet

Left Hand

FIGS. 1 & 2 Make a slip knot near end of yarn, leaving a short end. With crochet hook in left hand, held as you would hold a pencil, insert hook through slip knot stitch and tighten stitch on hook. Yarn is kept in the right hand, looped over forefinger and wrapped around little finger to adjust tension. The free end is held at base of stitch by thumb and forefinger.

CHAIN STITCH

FIGS. 3 & 4 Insert hook through slip knot stitch and under yarn strand on forefinger. Pull strand through stitch, making one chain stitch. Repeat directions for required number of chain stitches.

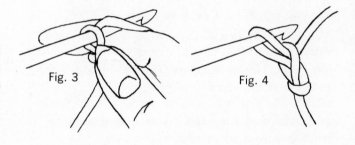

Fig. 3

Fig. 4

SINGLE CROCHET STITCH

FIG. 5 The single crochet is worked on a foundation row of chain stitches, as are all crochet stitches. Leave last chain completed on hook. Insert hook, front to back, under two top loops of second chain stitch from end, and under yarn strand. Pull yarn through loops, leaving two stitches on hook.

FIG. 6 Insert hook under yarn strand and pull through both stitches, leaving one stitch on hook.

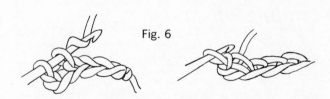

Fig. 6

Insert hook under two top loops of next chain stitch, and repeat directions. After last single crochet stitch of each row has been worked, chain one stitch before starting next row. On next and all following rows, begin single crochet stitch in *first* stitch on row below.

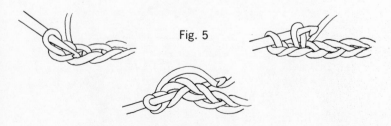

Fig. 5

knitting with two colors

When knitting with two yarns that are to be interchanged frequently across a row, hold one yarn in left hand and the other in the right hand. With the left-hand yarn, knit in the Continental Method (see p. 14 or 24), and knit as usual with the right-hand yarn. While one yarn is being worked, the other yarn must be carried *loosely* across the back of the fabric until it is needed. If the yarn being carried, the "floating yarn," is not loose, the fabric may pucker and the pattern be distorted.

NOTE: It is important to carry floating yarn across in the manner shown. Otherwise the front of the fabric will be incorrect.

If you wish to knit with the right hand only, drop one yarn strand and pick up the second from *under* the one just used, carrying the yarn not in use loosely across row.

KNIT

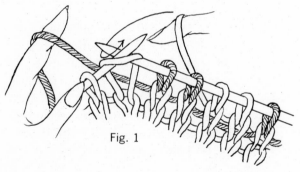

FIG. 1 Knit with right-hand yarn, stranding loose yarn under as shown.

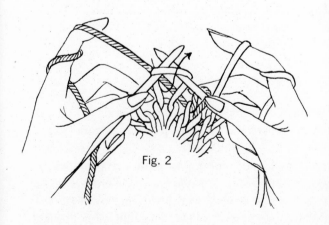

FIG. 2 Knit with left-hand yarn, stranding loose yarn above as shown.

PURL

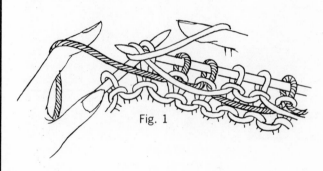

FIG. 1 Purl with right-hand yarn, stranding loose yarn under as shown.

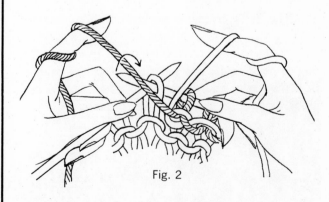

FIG. 2 Purl with left-hand yarn, stranding loose yarn above as shown.

Garter and Stockinette Stitches

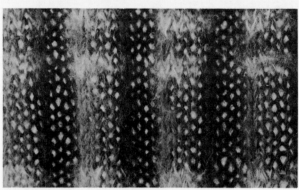

Ribbing

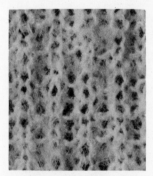

Rice Stitch

Seed Stitch

Butterfly Stitch

pattern stitches

GARTER STITCH

Any number of stitches. Knit every row. The Garter Stitch is shown opposite at top. Both sides of fabric look the same, and each ridge represents two rows.

STOCKINETTE STITCH

Any number of stitches. K 1 row, P 1 row. Repeat these two rows for pattern stitch. The front side of Stockinette fabric is shown opposite at bottom.

RIBBING

Even or Uneven number of stitches, depending on rib pattern chosen. Ribbing uses knit and purl stitches on same row. Various combinations of K and P stitches may be used to form different rib patterns, such as K 3, P 2, or, as shown. K 4, P 4. When working back side of fabric (wrong side facing you), the K stitches are purled and the P stitches are knit to maintain rib pattern on front.

SEED STITCH

Also called the Moss Stitch. Uneven number of stitches. * K 1, P 1, repeat from * across every row.

RICE STITCH

Even number of stitches. *Row 1, K. Row 2, * K 1, P 1, repeat from * across row. Repeat these two rows for pattern stitch.

BUTTERFLY STITCH

Multiple of 10 plus 5 (see p. 30). *Row 1, * Sl 5 holding yarn loosely to the front, K 5, repeat from * across row. *Row 2,* P. *Rows 3–12,* repeat Rows 1 & 2. *Row 13, * K 5, Sl 5 holding yarn loosely to the front, repeat from * across row. *Row 14,* P. *Rows 15–24,* repeat Rows 13 & 14. Repeat these 24 rows for pattern. After casting off, to make one butterfly: wrap 6 loose strands twice with a piece of yarn, bring ends of yarn through to wrong side and fasten. The size and position of the butterflies can be varied.

CABLE STITCH

Multiple of 12 plus 6 (see p. 30), *Row 1.* * P 2, K 2, P 2, K 6, repeat from * across row ending P 2, K 2, P 2. *Row 2,* K 2, P 2, K 2, * P 6, K 2, P 2, K 2, repeat from * across row. *3 & 5,* repeat Row 1. *4 & 6,* repeat Row 2. *Row 7,* * P 2, K 2, P 2, Sl 3 sts onto cable needle, and drop to front of work, K 3, K 3, from cable needle, repeat from * across row. Repeat Rows 2–7 for pattern. Size and position of cables can be varied. Drop needle to *back* of work to turn in opposite direction.

LACE STITCH

All lace patterns have YO and decrease as their basic stitches. The YO stitch creates a hole in the fabric when, on the alternate row, it is worked through the front side of the stitch (see p. 15 or 24). The pattern opposite is: Multiple of 12 plus 6. *Row 1,* * K 2 tog, YO, K 2, YO, K 2 tog, P 6, repeat from * across row. *Row 2,* * P 6, K 6, repeat from * across row. Repeat these two rows for pattern.

LEAFY LACE STITCH

Multiple of 6. (See p. 30) *Row 1,* * K 3 YO, K 3 tog, YO, repeat from * across row. *Row 2,* P. *Row 3,* repeat Row 1. *Row 4,* repeat Row 2. *Row 5,* * YO, K 3 tog, YO, K 3, repeat from * across row. *Row 6,* P. *Row 7,* repeat Row 5. *Row 8,* repeat Row 6. Repeat these eight rows for pattern.

CROSS STITCH (one over one)

One of the many cross stitch variations is: Uneven number of sts. *Row 1,* K 2, * Skip one st., take needle behind it and K second st., leaving it on needle, K first st. and slip both sts. off needle, repeat from * across row, ending K 1. *Row 2,* P 2, * Skip one st., P second st., leaving it on needle, P first st., slip both sts. off needle, repeat from * across row, ending P 1. Repeat these two rows for pattern.

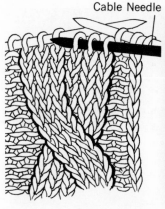

Cable Needle

Cable Stitch

Lace Stitch

Leafy Lace Stitch

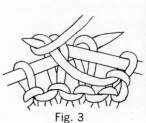

Cross Stitch

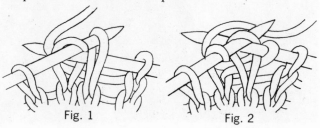

Fig. 1   Fig. 2   Fig. 3

how to create your own designs

I hope you will create your own knitting projects in addition to making the ones given in this book. You may plan your design before you begin or create it as you go along—many knitters prefer the latter (especially for wall hangings, see right) because the results are spontaneous and unique. But you must know pattern construction before making your own.

PATTERNS

Knitting instructions usually state that the pattern is made up of an Even or Uneven number of stitches, or that it requires a "MULTIPLE OF__" stitches, or a "MULTIPLE OF__PLUS__" stitches. These specifications indicate the number of stitches required for one pattern repeat. They aid you in adapting given directions to a different size, or in using the pattern in an original design.

If· a multiple of 12 stitches is required, then the number of pattern stitches worked must be evenly divisible by 12: 156, 168, 180, etc. When, as in Lace Stitch (p. 29) a multiple of 12 plus 6 stitches is required, 6 stitches are added: 162, 174, 186, etc. Another way to become familiar with pattern construction is through charting (see opposite page).

SAMPLERS

Make a sampler of many different patterns, working two rows of Garter Stitch between each pattern. Work at least two repeats of each pattern, both in width and in length. In this way you create a source of ideas for later projects, as well as becoming proficient at knitting many different pattern stitches.

Also make samplers of different yarns and combinations of yarns—to learn about them, what the stitch and row gauge will be with various sizes of needles in various patterns, and how yarns look when worked in various patterns. Knit with two dissimilar yarns as one strand, or combine very thick yarn with thin.

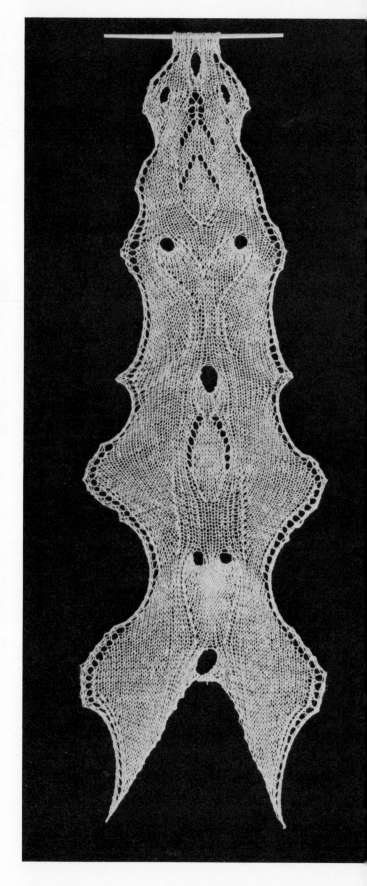

Wall hanging in linen, designed and knit by the author, uses a combination of stitches. Approximately 24″ long.

BEGINNING YOUR PROJECT

If you have obtained the gauge by making a sampler of your yarn in the pattern you have chosen, on the size needles you plan to use, you can easily obtain the number of stitches needed for the size you want. (Multiply the number of stitches you obtained per inch times the number of inches you require for the width of your project; repeat for rows.)

Then plan for the placement of your pattern repeats, making sure that the design will be evenly placed.

CHOOSING YOUR DESIGN

Refer to the samplers you have made to find a design and yarn you particularly like. Or, if you have decided upon a design or a yarn that you are unfamiliar with, work a new sampler of not less than two pattern repeats to obtain the stitch and row gauge. When choosing a pattern, remember that a complicated pattern will not usually show up very well when worked with a "busy" yarn. Also, consider how the item is to be used—a Lace Stitch will not make a sturdy rug fabric.

COLOR

When the right shades are chosen, almost any color combination is possible. Consider each yarn in relation to the others to be used in your project. Look to nature for ideas—so many different colors are combined in a single flower petal, in fish scales, butterfly wings, bird feathers, stones, etc. Here again

you will profit from making samplers.

Patterns may be created on the simplest knitting stitch through use of color alone. And using your imagination in combining leftover yarns will lead you to unusual designs.

PATTERN CHARTS

Most likely you have seen pattern charts of color designs for ski sweaters and the like. But charts are used in some knitting books for stitch patterns. A general knowledge of charts will help you in creating your own designs, and you will also be able to reproduce a pattern which you see in a knit fabric for which you have no written specifications.

A chart of a pattern gives the same information as the written specifications discussed before, and it also tells you how to work the pattern. It does this by means of symbols.

Charting is done on squared-off paper such as graph paper. Each square equals one stitch and each line represents one row or round. The chart shows the front side of the fabric. When making up a chart or when working from one, read it from bottom to top, from right to left for Row 1 (front side facing), and from left to right for Row 2 (back side facing).

It is best to plan more than one repeat of the pattern, in width and in length. Make up your own symbols to represent different kinds of stitches, or yarns—or use colored pencils.

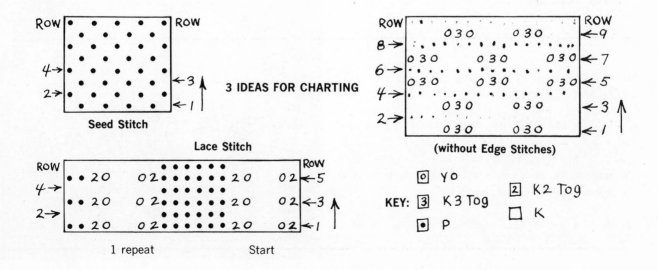

3 IDEAS FOR CHARTING

Seed Stitch

Lace Stitch

1 repeat   Start

(without Edge Stitches)

KEY: ○ Y O   ③ K 3 Tog   ② K 2 Tog   □ K   ● P

helpful hints

DROPPED STITCHES

FIGS. 1 & 2 To pick up dropped *knit* stitches (Fig. 1), use crochet hook to work loose stitch up ladder of strands. Insert hook into loose stitch front to back, catch strand and pull through stitch.

To pick up dropped *purl* stitches (Fig. 2), crochet hook must be reinserted through stitch front to back after each new stitch has been formed.

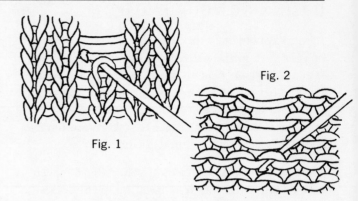

Fig. 1

Fig. 2

RIPPED STITCHES

To pick up knit (Fig. 3) and purl (Fig. 4) stitches after ripping, be careful to insert needle through stitch as shown to prevent twisting.

If you are ripping one stitch at a time, insert needle back to front into ripped stitch so that it will not be twisted.

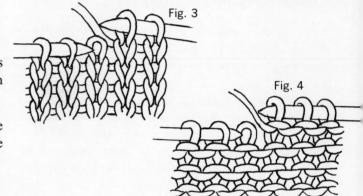

Fig. 3

Fig. 4

PICKING UP STITCHES

To pick up stitches along an edge, hold right side of work facing you, insert needle through loops on edge and draw yarn through, forming one stitch. Repeat for the desired number of stitches, being careful to have the picked up stitches evenly distributed along the edge.

Fig. 5

JOINING YARN

Yarns should be joined at the beginning or end of a row, not in the middle of the fabric. Leave ends of a few inches of new and old yarn below joining, to be woven into wrong side of fabric with a tapestry needle or crochet hook.

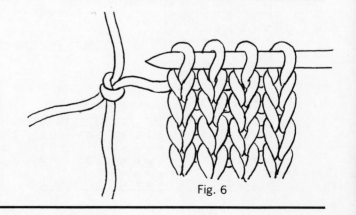

Fig. 6

DOUBLE POINTED NEEDLES (dp)

FIGS. 1 & 2 Cast on required number of stitches onto one needle and divide stitches onto three needles as directed. When working first row, be careful not to twist stitches as you go from one needle to the next. Last stitch of first row is linked to first stitch (Fig. 2), thus joining the three needles.

CIRCULAR NEEDLES

FIG. 3 Circular needles may be used for straight knitting as well as circular. When working straight on a circular needle, work back and forth across rows. They are recommended especially for large projects such as stoles and blankets, because the weight of the work rests in your lap and your arms do not become overly tired. Another advantage to circular knitting needles is that there are no needle ends to catch on the arms of chairs.

Color photographs of related projects precede individual instructions.

MARKERS

FIG 4 Markers are useful in separating border stitches from pattern stitches. Knit border stitches, slip marker onto needle, and work pattern stitches, putting another marker before end border. They will serve as a reminder when you work across each row.

SEWING SEAMS

Fabrics are joined *after* blocking. Pin pieces together before sewing. Use a tapestry needle threaded with a strand of your yarn and sew with an over hand stitch, being careful not to sew too tightly. You may also crochet fabrics together with SC, again being careful not to work too tightly.

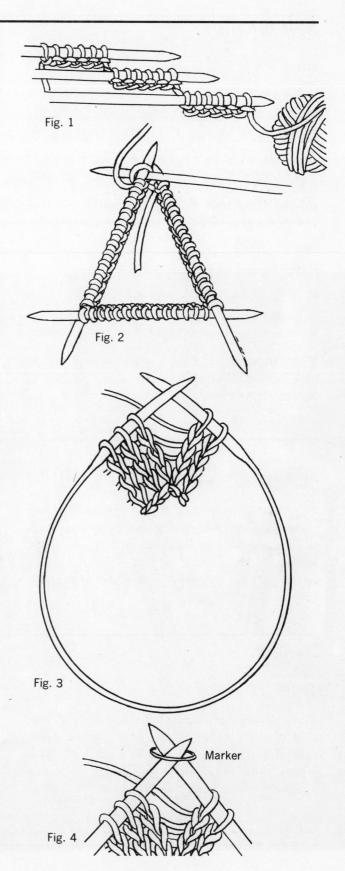

Fig. 1

Fig. 2

Fig. 3

Marker

Fig. 4

scarves

Scarves are practical additions to any wardrobe. The two shown are very easy to make. The blue and gold scarf is comfortable and lightweight, with a wonderfully spongy texture and much warmth provided by the open quality of the pattern stitch. ■ Tighter in knit and of heavier weight, the sporty red, black, and white striped scarf is made with the Garter Stitch.

scarves

BLUE & GOLD SCARF

this scarf is shown on page 34

SIZE: 11 inches by 48 inches before fringe

MATERIALS: Columbia-Minerva Corp., 2-oz. skeins
Featherweight Worsted:
　　#640 Antique Gold Heather　　1 skein
　　#644 Thistle Blue Heather　　2 skeins
Suggested needle size: no. 8; English no. 5

GAUGE: 3½ sts = 1 inch

PATTERN STITCH: Uneven number of sts (see p. 28)
* K 1 into row below, P 1, repeat from * across
every row for pattern stitch. See p. 65.

DIRECTIONS: Cast on 39 sts with Blue. K 1 row. Work
in pattern stitch:

Blue:	4 inches	Gold:	1 inch
Gold:	3 inches	Blue:	1 inch
Blue:	1 inch	Gold:	1 inch
Gold:	1 inch	Blue:	1 inch
Blue:	1 inch	Gold:	3 inches
Gold:	1 inch	Blue:	4 inches
Blue:	26 inches	Cast off. Block.

Add fringe of Gold yarn.

STRIPED SCARF

this scarf is shown on page 35

SIZE: 12 inches by 60 inches before fringe

MATERIALS: Columbia-Minerva Corp., 1-oz. skeins
Sayelle Nantuk sports yarn;
　　#5312　　Black　　3 skeins
　　#5314　　Persian Tile　　3 skeins
　　#5332　　Winter White　　3 skeins
Suggested needle size: no. 7; English no. 6

GAUGE: 5 sts = 1 inch

PATTERN STITCH: Garter Stitch

DIRECTIONS: Cast on 60 sts with Persian Tile. K 6
rows. * K 3 rows with White, K 3 rows with Black,
K 3 rows with Persian Tile. Repeat from * until
scarf measures 59 inches. K 6 rows with Persian
Tile. Cast off. No blocking is necessary. Fringe: cut
three 12-inch lengths of yarn for each fringe; alternate fringes of each color, tying one fringe into
every other st.

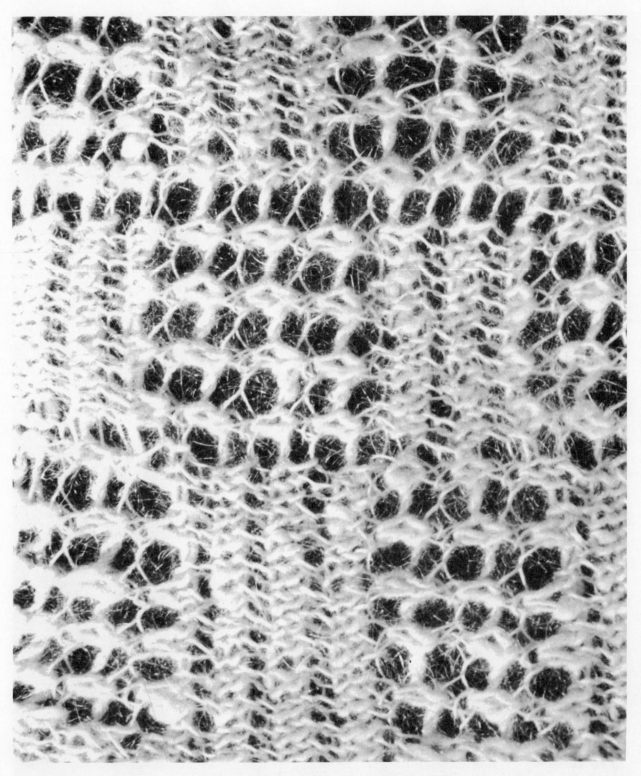

Detail of mohair and wool blanket with a lacelike effect, designed and knit by
the author. Making sample swatches is the best way to develop your own ideas.

scarves

The striped scarf of aqua, apricot, and beige is knit on the bias. It is worked in a combination of Lace and Garter Stitches. ■ The white scarf is made with mohair and wool yarn. It is worked in the Rice Stitch, a combination of knit and purl stitches, and is extremely simple to make. This is definitely a scarf for the beginner.

STRIPED SCARF

this scarf is shown on page 38

SIZE: 9½ inches by 65 inches before fringe

MATERIALS: Pauline Denham Yarns, Inc., 50-gram
balls

Joli	#23	Miel	1 ball
Joli	#975	Aqua	1 ball
Joli	#1002	Oz	1 ball

Suggested needle size: no. 8; English no. 8

GAUGE: 4 sts = 1 inch; 4½ rows = 1 inch

PATTERN STITCH: This is a bias pattern. Lace and
Garter stitches

Row 1, K 1, YO, K across, ending K 2 tog.
Row 2, K across, K into back of YO st.
Row 3, K 1, YO, K 1, *YO, K 2 tog, repeat from *
across, ending K 1, K 2 tog.
Row 4, K across, K into back of *last* YO st *only*.

DIRECTIONS: Cast on 51 sts with Miel.
*Miel: Work pattern Rows 1 & 2; work Rows 1
through 4 three times; work Rows 1 & 2.
Oz: Work Rows 1 & 2; work Rows 1 through 4
three times; work Rows 1 & 2.
Aqua: Work Rows 1 & 2; work Rows 1 through 4
three times; work Rows 1 & 2.
Miel: Work Rows 1 & 2 six times.
Oz: Work Rows 1 & 2 six times.
Aqua: Work Rows 1 & 2 six times.
Repeat from * twice more.
Miel: Work Rows 1 & 2; work Rows 1 through 4
three times: work Rows 1 & 2.
Oz: Work Rows 1 & 2; work Rows 1 through 4
three times; work Rows 1 & 2.
Aqua: Work Rows 1 & 2; work Rows 1 through 4
three times; work Rows 1 & 2.

Cast off. Block. Fringe: Aqua fringe at Aqua edge,
Miel at other edge.

WHITE SCARF

this scarf is shown on page 39

SIZE: 14½ inches by 60 inches before fringe

MATERIALS: William Unger & Co., Inc., 40-gram and
50-gram balls

Saltarelle	#27	White	2 balls
Mohair de luxe	#39	White	2 balls
Musette	#505	White	1 ball

Suggested needle size: no. 8; English no. 5
Crochet hook: no. 5

GAUGE: 5 sts = 1 inch

PATTERN STITCH: Rice Stitch. Even number of sts
Row 1, K.
Row 2, * K 1, P 1, repeat from * across row.
Repeat these 2 rows for pattern stitch.

DIRECTIONS: Cast on 60 sts with Saltarelle. Work Row
1 of pattern. Change to Musette and work Row 2 of
pattern. Change to Mohair and repeat Row 1. Change
to Saltarelle and repeat Row 2. Continue in pattern
stitch, alternating yarn every row in above order,
until scarf measures 60 inches. Cast off. With SC,
crochet across each end of scarf. Block. Fringe: cut
12-inch lengths of yarn for fringe, using one length
of Musette and one of Saltarelle for each fringe. Tie
fringe into every other SC stitch.

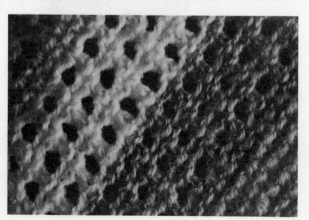

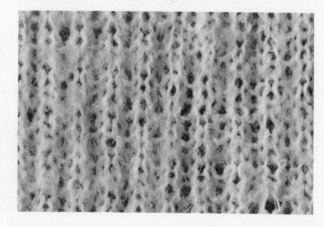

Contemporary wool sock from Yugoslavia illustrates an effective use of stranded knitting. Brooklyn Museum.

stoles

The yellow stole is worked in a Lace Stitch. Because mohair yarn is used, the stole is soft and fluffy. ■ The blue and purple stole is worked in a bias Lace Stitch with chevron edges. The purple yarn is a tweed yarn. ■ For those allergic to wool, the green striped stole is recommended because the yarn used is synthetic. This yarn is available in a wide variety of colors. ■ These stoles may be knit on circular needles, which make it easier to handle the large number of stitches. Work back and forth across the rows.

stoles

YELLOW STOLE

this stole is shown on page 42

SIZE: 26 inches by 68 inches before fringe

MATERIALS: William Unger & Co., Inc., 40-gram balls
Mohair de luxe #52 Yellow 8 balls
Suggested needle size: no. 9; English no 4

Circular Crochet hook

GAUGE: 3 sts = 1 inch; 5 rows = 1 inch

PATTERN STITCH: Multiple of 12 plus 6
* K 6, YO, K 2 tog, YO, K 2 tog, YO, K 2 tog,
repeat from * across row, ending K 6.
Repeat this row for pattern stitch.

DIRECTIONS: Cast on 78 sts. K 2 rows. Work even in pattern stitch until 7 balls of yarn have been used. K 2 rows and cast off. Crochet one row of SC across each end of stole. Block. Fringe: cut two 12-inch lengths of yarn for each fringe; tie into every third SC st.

BLUE AND PURPLE STOLE

this stole is shown on page 42

SIZE: 19 inches by 58 inches before fringe

MATERIALS: Spinnerin Yarn Co., Inc.
Gaelic Tweed #71 Donegal Blue
6 balls (50-gram balls)
Frostlon Petite #124 Skipper Blue
5 balls (1-oz. balls)
Suggested needle size: no. 10½ circular; English no. 2

GAUGE: 3½ sts = 1 inch

PATTERN STITCH: Multiple of 8 plus 5
Row 1, K 2, * K 1, YO, K 2, P 3 tog, K 2, YO, repeat from *, ending K 3.
Row 2, P.
Repeat these 2 rows for pattern stitch.

DIRECTIONS: Frostlon Petite is worked with double strand throughout. Cast on 61 sts with Gaelic Tweed, and work in pattern stitch for 4 rows. *Change to Frostlon Petite and work in pattern stitch for 2 rows. Change to Gaelic Tweed and work in pattern stitch for 2 rows. Repeat from * for 132 rows. End with Gaelic Tweed, working 4 rows of pattern stitch. Cast off. Crochet one row of SC across both ends. Block. Fringe: cut two 12-inch lengths of each yarn for each fringe; tie into SC st at each point.

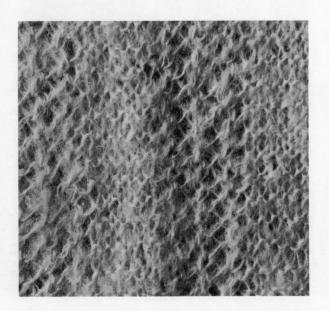

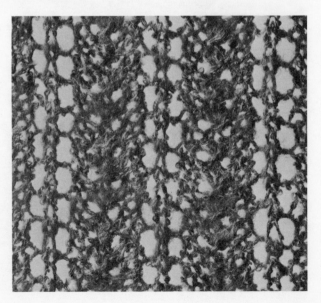

GREEN STRIPED STOLE

this stole is shown on page 43

SIZE: 22 inches by 60 inches before fringe

MATERIALS: The American Thread Co., 2-oz. skeins
    Mohspun #533 Winter Grass   2 skeins
    Mohspun #533 Lime Mist   2 skeins
    Suggested needle size: no. 10; English no. 3

GAUGE: 3 sts = 1 inch; 5 rows = 1 inch

PATTERN STITCH: Ribbing. Multiple of 8 plus 4

DIRECTIONS: Use double strand of yarn throughout. Cast on 68 sts with Winter Grass. In K 4, P 4 ribbing, work:

*Winter Grass:	8 rows
Lime:	2 rows
Winter Grass:	2 rows
Lime:	2 rows
Winter Grass:	2 rows
Lime:	8 rows

Repeat from * nine times more.

Winter Grass:	2 rows
Lime:	2 rows
Winter Grass:	8 rows

Cast off. Block. Fringe: use Lime fringe at both ends.

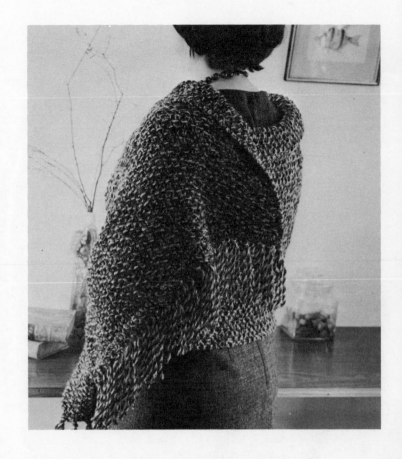

BLACK, GRAY, AND RUST STOLE

this stole is shown above

SIZE: 21½ inches by 72 inches before fringe

MATERIALS: William Unger & Co., Inc., 50-gram balls
    Poncho Cablee #184 12 balls
    Suggested needle size: no. 15 circular;
      English no. 000
    Crochet hook: size J (aluminum)

GAUGE: 2½ sts = 1 inch

PATTERN STITCH: Seed Stitch. Uneven number of sts

  * K 1, P 1, repeat from * across every row for pattern stitch.

DIRECTIONS: Cast on 51 sts. Work in pattern stitch until 11 balls of yarn have been used. Cast off. Crochet one row of SC across each end of stole. Block. Fringe: cut two 12-inch lengths of yarn for each fringe; tie into every other SC st.

pillows

Add a burst of bright yellow to a sofa or chair, or reverse the pillow to display its white side. Make several of these pillows in different shades to blend with your own color scheme. This is an excellent project for leftover yarns. Both sides are knit in the Leaf Pattern Stitch, a type of Lace Stitch. ■ The striped pillow on this page is worked in the Garter Stitch. You can make several of these at a time since it is easy and fast knitting.

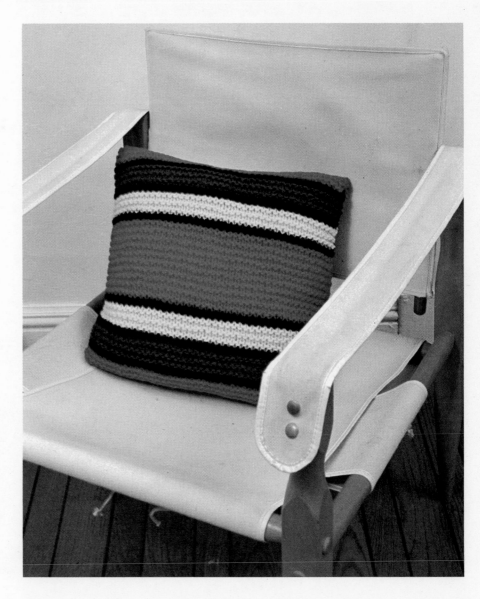

pillows

YELLOW AND WHITE PILLOW

this pillow is shown on page 46

SIZE: 10 inches by 14 inches

MATERIALS: Diamond Yarn Corp., 50-gram balls
        Levikka Sport Yarn #60 Yellow   1 ball
        Levikka Sport Yarn #61 White   1 ball
        Suggested needle size: no. 8; English no. 5

GAUGE: 3½ sts = 1 inch

PATTERN STITCH: Lace Stitch. Multiple of 6 plus 4
   Row 1, K 2, * K 3, YO, K 3 tog, YO, repeat
   from * across row, ending K 2.
   Row 2, P.
   Row 3, K 2, * YO, K 3 tog, YO, K 3, repeat from
   * across row, ending K 2.
   Row 4, P.

DIRECTIONS: **Front:** Cast on 49 sts with Yellow. Work
in Stockinette Stitch for 4 rows. * Work pattern
Rows 1 & 2 twice. Work pattern Rows 3 & 4 twice.
Repeat from * four times more. Work pattern
Rows 1 & 2. Work in Stockinette Stitch for 4 rows
and cast off. **Back:** With White, repeat directions
for Front. Block. With right sides facing, sew sides
together, leaving one side open to insert pillow. Turn
right side out, insert pillow, and sew fourth side.

STRIPED PILLOW

this pillow is shown on page 47

SIZE: 15 inches square

MATERIALS: Emile Bernat & Sons Co., 1-oz. skeins
   Craftsmens Rug Wool #3148 Vermillion   6 skeins
   Craftsmens Rug Wool #3153 Gobelen Blue 1 skein
   Craftsmens Rug Wool #3155 Black   1 skein
   Craftsmens Rug Wool #3173 Cream   1 skein
   Suggested needle size: no. 11

GAUGE: 3 sts = 1 inch

PATTERN STITCH: Garter Stitch

DIRECTIONS: **Front:** Cast on 45 sts with Vermillion.
Work in Garter Stitch using the following color
pattern:

Vermil:	6 rows	Vermil:	20 rows
Black:	2 rows	Black:	2 rows
Blue:	6 rows	Cream:	6 rows
Black:	2 rows	Black:	2 rows
Cream:	6 rows	Blue:	6 rows
Black:	2 rows	Black:	2 rows
		Vermil:	6 rows

Cast off. **Back:** Cast on 45 sts with Red. K 66 rows.
Cast off. Block both pieces. With right sides facing,
sew three sides together. Turn right side out, insert
pillow and sew fourth side.

The narrow multicolored pillow is made of odds and ends of yarn, a good project for experimenting with your leftover yarns. ■ *In addition to the check design in the black and white pillow, an unusual texture is created through a subtle combination of knit and purl stitches. It is knit with wool and cotton.* ■ *The beige pillow uses the Butterfly Stitch on the front side. It is made with a variegated yarn which is thick and loose-spun, giving a soft and cozy quality to the knit.*

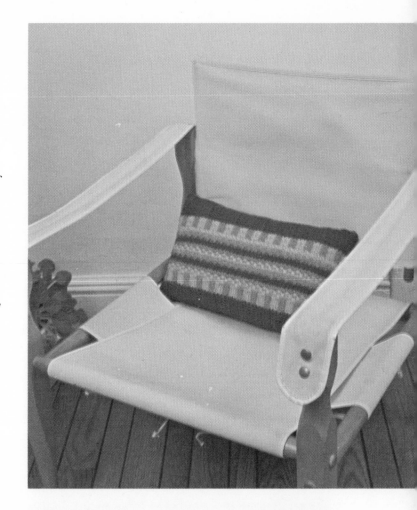

BRIGHT BLUE AND PINK PILLOW

This pillow is shown on page 49

SIZE: 9½ inches by 15 inches

MATERIALS: 4 ply knitting worsted

Bright Blue	4 oz.
Bright Pink	2 oz.
Bright Orange	2 oz.

Suggested needle size: no. 10½; English no. 2

One pillow 9½ inches by 15 inches

GAUGE: 3 sts = 1 inch; 4 rows = 1 inch

PATTERN STITCH: Combination Stockinette, Ribbing, and Seed Stitches (see p. 28)

DIRECTIONS: Use double strand of yarn throughout.

Front: Cast on 52 sts with Blue, and work as follows:

Blue: work in K 4, P 4 ribbing for 8 rows.

Pink & Orange: * K 2 with Pink K 2 with Orange, repeat from * across row.
* P 2 with Orange, P 2 with Pink, repeat from * across row.
Repeat these two rows once more.

Pink: work 2 rows Seed Stitch (K 1, P 1 across first row, P 1, K 1 across next row).

Orange: work 2 rows Seed Stitch.

Blue: work 2 rows Stockinette Stitch.

Orange: work 2 rows Seed Stitch.

Pink: work 2 rows Seed Stitch.

Orange: work 2 rows Seed Stitch.

Blue: work 2 rows Stockinette Stitch.

Orange: work 2 rows Seed Stitch.

Pink: work 2 rows Seed Stitch.

Pink & Orange: * K 2 with Pink K 2 with Orange, repeat from * across row.
* P 2 with Orange, P 2 with Pink, repeat from * across row.
Repeat these two rows once more.

Blue: work in K 4, P 4 ribbing for 8 rows.

Cast off. **Back:** Cast on 52 sts with Blue. Work in Stockinette Stitch until piece measures 9 inches. Cast off. Block both pieces. With right sides facing, sew pieces together, leaving one side open to insert pillow. Turn right side out, insert pillow and sew fourth side.

BLACK AND WHITE PILLOW

this pillow is shown on page 49

SIZE: 11 inches square

MATERIALS: Coats & Clark, Inc., 1-oz. skeins
Red Heart knitting worsted E. 232
#1 White 1 skein
#12 Black 3 skeins
Pearl Cotton C. 19 #1 White 1 ball
Pearl Cotton C. 19 #12 Black 3 balls
Suggested needle size: no. 7; English no. 6

GAUGE: **Front:** 4½ sts = 1 inch; **Back:** 4 sts = 1 inch

PATTERN STITCH: Combination Knit and Purl. Even number of sts

DIRECTIONS: Wool and cotton are knit together. **Front:** Cast on 50 sts with Black. **Row 1,** * K 2 with Black, K 2 with White, repeat from * across row. **Row 2,** * P 2 with Black, K 2 with White, repeat from * across row. **Row 3,** * K 2 with White, K 2 with Black, repeat from * across row. **Row 4,** * K 2 with White, P 2 with Black, repeat from * across row. Repeat these four rows 12 times more. Repeat rows 1 & 2 once. Cast off with Black. **Back:** Cast on 45 sts with Black. Work in Stockinette Stitch until back measures same size as front. Cast off. Block both pieces to 11¼ inches. With right sides facing, sew three sides together. Turn right side out, insert pillow, and sew fourth side.

BEIGE PILLOW

this pillow is shown on page 49

SIZE: 14 inches square

MATERIALS: Pauline Denham Yarns, Inc., 2-oz, skeins
Kensington #1208 Curry Beige 5 skeins
Suggested needle size: no. 10; English no. 3
Crochet hook size J (metal)

GAUGE: 3½ sts = 1 inch

PATTERN STITCH: Butterfly Stitch (see p. 28). Multiple of 10 plus 4
Row 1, K 2, * Sl 5 holding yarn loosely to front, K 5, repeat from * across row, ending Sl 5, K 2.
Row 2, P.
Row 3, K 2, * K 5, Sl 5 holding yarn loosely to the front, repeat from * across row, ending K 7.
Row 4, P.

DIRECTIONS: **Front:** Cast on 49 sts. K 1 row, P 1 row. Work pattern Rows 1 & 2 six times. Work Rows 3 & 4 six times. Work Rows 1 & 2 six times. Work Rows 3 & 4 six times. Work Rows 1 & 2 six times. K 1 row and cast off. Work butterflies on front: wrap 6 loose strands twice with piece of yarn, bring ends of yarn through to wrong side and fasten. **Back:** Cast on 49 sts. Work in Stockinette Stitch until piece measures 13½ inches. Cast off. Block both pieces. With wrong sides facing, and front of pillow facing you, crochet three sides together with SC. Insert pillow and crochet fourth side.

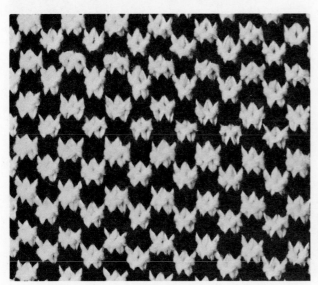

floor pillows

These pillows are made with rug wool which is sturdy and requires little care. The honeycomb pillow has stripes on the reverse side, as shown on the opposite page, top right. You may wish to use one pattern for both sides of the pillow. ■ Slightly smaller, the diagonally striped pillow is knit in a combination of Stockinette and Garter Stitches. It is worked from corner to corner.

HONEYCOMB FLOOR PILLOW

this pillow is shown on pages 52 and 53

SIZE: 22 inches square

MATERIALS: Paterneyan Yarn Co., approx. 3½-oz. skeins

Persian Rug Yarn #221	Plum	1 skein
Persian Rug Yarn #242	Red	1 skein
Persian Rug Yarn #424	Orange	1 skein
Persian Rug Yarn #610	Mauve	1 skein
Persian Rug Yarn #821	Cerese	1 skein
Persian Rug Yarn #827	Pink	1 skein

Suggested needle size: no. 6 (English no. 7) circular for front, no. 5 (English no. 8) for back

Crochet hook: size J

GAUGE: 4 sts = 1 inch; 6 rows = 1 inch

PATTERN STITCH: Multiple of 8 plus 6

Row 1, K 2, *Sl 2 sts, K 6, repeat from * across row, ending Sl 2, K 2.

Row 2, P 2, *Sl 2 sts, P 6, repeat from * across row, ending Sl 2, P 2.

Row 3, K 6, * Sl 2 sts, K 6, repeat from * across row.

Row 4, P 6, * Sl 2 sts, P 6, repeat from * across row.

DIRECTIONS: **Front:** Cast on 92 sts with Plum. K 4 rows.

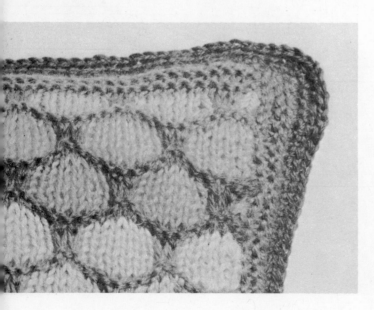

Orange: work pattern Rows 1 & 2 twice.
*Plum: K 2 rows.
Pink: work pattern Rows 3 & 4 three times.
Mauve: K 2 rows.
Red: work pattern Rows 1 & 2 three times.
Mauve: K 2 rows.
Cerese: work pattern Rows 3 & 4 three times.
Plum: K 2 rows.
Orange: work pattern Rows 1 & 2 three times.
Repeat from * three times more.
Plum: K 2 rows.
Pink: work pattern Rows 3 & 4 three times.
Mauve: K 2 rows.
Red: work pattern Rows 1 & 2 three times.
Mauve: K 2 rows.
Cerese: work pattern Rows 3 & 4 three times.
Plum: K 2 rows.
Orange: work pattern Rows 1 & 2 twice.
Plum: K 4 rows

Cast off. With front side facing you, on circular needle pick up 88 sts on right edge with Plum. K 4 rows and cast off. Repeat for left edge. With Mauve, crochet one row in SC around the 4 sides.

Back: Cast on 84 sts with Orange.
Orange: work 4 rows Stockinette.
Plum: K 2 rows.
*Pink: work 6 rows Stockinette.
Mauve: K 2 rows.
Red: work 6 rows Stockinette.
Mauve: K 2 rows.
Cerese: work 6 rows Stockinette.
Plum: K 2 rows.
Orange: work 4 rows Stockinette.
Plum: K 2 rows.
Repeat from * three times more.
Pink: work 6 rows Stockinette.
Mauve: K 2 rows.
Red: work 6 rows Stockinette.
Mauve: K 2 rows.
Cerese: work 6 rows Stockinette.
Plum: K 2 rows.
Orange: work 4 rows Stockinette.

Cast off. Block both pieces. (The stripes on back of pillow run in opposite direction from stripes on front). With wrong sides together and with front side facing you, with Mauve crochet three sides together with SC. Insert pillow and crochet fourth side.

STOCKINETTE FLOOR PILLOW

this pillow is shown on page 53

SIZE: 20 inches square

MATERIALS: Paterneyan Yarn Co.
Pat Rug Yarn #010 White   1 lb.
Pat Rug Yarn #511 Brown   ½ lb.
Pat Rug Yarn #610 Eggplant ½ lb.
Suggested needle size: no. 10½ circular;
English no. 2
Crochet hook: size J

GAUGE: 2½ sts = 1 inch; 4 rows = 1 inch

PATTERN STITCH: **Row 1**, K 1, YO, K across row, ending YO, K 1.
Row 2, P.
Row 3, P 1, YO, P across row, ending YO, P 1.
Row 4, K.
Row 5, K 2 tog, K across row, ending K 2 tog.
Row 6, P 2 tog, P across row, ending P 2 tog.

DIRECTIONS: **Front**: Cast on 2 sts with Brown, and work as follows:

Brown: work pattern Rows 1 & 2 until there are 33 sts on needle, ending with Row 2.
White: work pattern Rows 1 & 2 until there are 39 sts on needle, ending with Row 2.
Brown: work pattern Rows 1 & 4.
Eggplant: work pattern Rows 1 & 4; work Rows 3 & 4 until there are 49 sts on needle, ending with Row 4.
White: work pattern Rows 1 & 4.
Brown: work pattern Rows 1 & 4.
Eggplant: work pattern Rows 1 & 4.
White: work pattern Rows 1 & 4.
Brown: work pattern Rows 1 & 4.
Eggplant: work pattern Rows 1 & 4.
White: work pattern Rows 1 & 4.
Brown: work pattern Rows 1 & 4.
Eggplant: work pattern Rows 1 & 4 until there are 69 sts on needle, ending with Row 4; work Rows 5 & 4 in that order until there are 65 sts on needle, ending with Row 4.
Brown: work pattern Rows 5 & 4 in that order.
White: work pattern Rows 5 & 4 in that order.
Eggplant: work pattern Rows 5 & 4 in that order.
Brown: work pattern Rows 5 & 4 in that order.

White: work pattern Rows 5 & 4 in that order.
Eggplant: work pattern Rows 5 & 4 in that order.
Brown: work pattern Rows 5 & 4 in that order.
White: work pattern Rows 5 & 4 in that order.
Eggplant: work pattern Rows 6 & 4 until there are 43 sts on needle, ending with Row 4; work Rows 5 & 4 in that order.
Brown: work pattern Rows 5 & 4 in that order.
White: work pattern Rows 5 & 2 in that order until there are 33 sts on needle, ending with Row 2.
Brown: work pattern Rows 5 & 2 in that order until there are 3 sts on needle, ending with Row 2; Sl 1, K 2 tog, PSSO, pull yarn through remaining st.

With SC, crochet with Brown around 4 sides of pillow. Block. **Back**: Cast on 2 sts with Brown. Work pattern Rows 1 & 2 until there are 69 sts on needle, ending with Row 2. Work pattern Rows 5 & 2 in that order until 3 sts remain on needle, ending with Row 2. Sl 1, K 2 tog, PSSO, pull yarn through remaining st. Block. With right sides facing, sew pieces together, leaving one side open to insert pillow. Turn right side out, insert pillow, and sew fourth side.

blankets

The emerald, white, and blue stripe blanket is worked in the Lace-Cable Stitch. Made of mohair, it is lightweight and very fluffy. ■ *The red blanket is one of the simplest to make—definitely good for the beginner. The Fuzilli and Scandia yarns give the blanket a spongy texture of medium weight.* ■ *All blanket projects given here are one-piece knitting. You will probably find it easier to knit them on circular needles, working back and forth across the rows.*

blankets

EMERALD, WHITE, AND BLUE BLANKET

this blanket is shown on page 56

SIZE: 54 inches by 68 inches, including crochet edge

MATERIALS: Coats & Clark, Inc., 40-gram skeins
    Mohcora #E291 #1 White   7 skeins
    Mohcora #E291 #676 Emerald 7 skeins
    Mohcora #E291 #848 Skipper Blue 7 skeins
    Suggested needle size: no. 8 circular; English no. 5
    Crochet hook: size H
    Cable needle

GAUGE: 3½ sts = 1 inch; 4 rows = 1 inch (measure Stockinette Stitch).

PATTERN STITCH: Lace-Cable Stitch. Multiple of 12 plus 10

Row 1, Blue sts: K 4, P 2, * K 6, P 2, K 2, P 2, repeat from * 4 times in all, ending K 6, P 2, K 2;
White sts: K 2, P 2, * K 6, P 2, K 2, P 2, repeat from * 4 times in all, ending K 6, P 2, K 2;
Emerald sts: K 2, P 2, * K 6, P 2, K 2, P 2, repeat from * 4 times in all, ending K 6, P 2, K 4.
Row 2, Emerald sts: P 4, K 2, P 6, * K 2, P 2, K 2, P 6, repeat from * 4 times in all, ending K 2, P 2;
White sts: P 2, K 2, P 6, * K 2, P 2, K 2, P 6, repeat from * 4 times in all, ending K 2, P 2;

Blue sts: P 2, K 2, P 6, * K 2, P 2, K 2, P 6, repeat from * 4 times in all, ending K 2, P 4.
Row 3, Blue sts: K 4, P 2, * turn cable in next 6 sts (Sl 3 sts onto cable needle and drop to front of work, K 3 sts, K 3 sts from cable needle), P 2, K 2, P 2, repeat from * 4 times in all, ending turn cable in 6 sts, P 2, K 2;
White sts: continue ribbing pattern, turning cable in every K 6 rib;
Emerald sts: continue ribbing pattern, turning cable in every K 6 rib; ending K 4.
Row 4, repeat Row 2
Row 5, Blue sts: K 4, P 2, * K 2 tog, YO, K 2, YO, K 2 tog, P 2, K 2, P 2, repeat from * 4 times in all, ending P 2, K 2;
White sts: K 2, P 2, * K 2 tog, YO, K 2, YO, K 2 tog, P 2, K 2, P 2, repeat from * 4 times in all, ending P 2, K 2;
Emerald sts: K 2, P 2, * K 2 tog, YO, K 2, YO, K 2 tog, P 2, K 2, P 2, repeat from * 4 times in all, ending P 2, K 4.
Row 6, repeat Row 2.

DIRECTIONS: Cast on 190 sts, 64 with Emerald, 62 with White, 64 with Blue. Work pattern Rows 1 & 2 for 8 rows. * Work pattern Rows 3 & 4 once. Work pattern Rows 5 & 6 for 8 rows. Repeat from * 20 times more. Work pattern Rows 3 & 4. Work pattern Rows 1 & 2 for 8 rows. Cast off. Crochet 2 rows SC around all 4 sides, using Blue yarn on Blue edges, White on White, and Emerald on Emerald. Block.

RED BLANKET

this blanket is shown on page 57

SIZE: 50 inches by 66 inches

MATERIALS: Emile Bernat & Sons Co., 2-oz. skeins

| Scandia | #6033 | Vermillion | 11 skeins |
| Fuzilli | #8333 | Vermillion | 10 skeins |

Suggested needle size: no. 15 circular;
English no. 000
Crochet hook: size 13 (wooden)

GAUGE: 4½ sts = 2 inches

PATTERN STITCH: Alternate 4 rows of Garter Stitch with 4 rows of Stockinette Stitch for pattern stitch.

DIRECTIONS: With Scandia, cast on 110 sts and K 2 rows. * With Fuzilli, K 4 rows, leaving 7 inches of yarn at beginning of first row and at end of last row (to be used for fringe). With Scandia work in Stockinette Stitch for 4 rows. Repeat from * 24 times in all. With Fuzilli, K 4 rows, leaving 7 inches of yarn at edges as before. With Scandia, K 2 rows. Cast off. With SC, crochet across both ends of blanket. Block. Fringe: two 12-inch lengths of Fuzilli are used for each fringe on left side of blanket, one 12-inch length for each fringe is added to ends on right side.

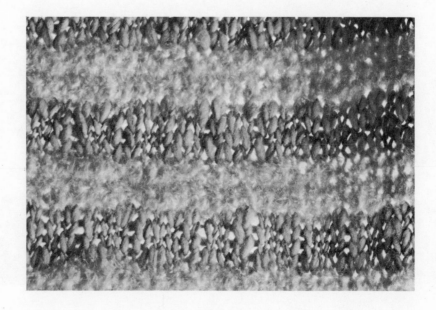

blankets

The green striped blanket is knit in a chevron pattern, using the Lace Stitch. ■ *The afghan shown below was made by Mrs. John Axford Higgons for her son before World War I. The patches depict various flags as well as emblems of her son's schools, college, and fraternity. An example of creating your own design.*

CHEVRON STRIPED BLANKET

this blanket is shown on page 60

SIZE: 50 inches by 72 inches

MATERIALS: Bear Brand-Fleishers, 4-oz. skeins
    Superior Knitting Worsted
      #173   Charcoal   3 skeins
    Superior Knitting Worsted #460
      #460   Olive   2 skeins
    Superior Knitting Worsted #466
      #466   Celery   3 skeins
    Suggested needle size: no. 8 circular;
    English no. 5

GAUGE: 4 sts = 1 inch

PATTERN STITCH: Lace Stitch. Multiple of 14 plus 7
Row 1, K 3, * K 1, YO, K 5, P 3 tog, K 5, YO, repeat from * across row, ending K 4.
Row 2, P.
Row 3, repeat Row 1.
Row 4, P across, P into *back* of YO sts.

DIRECTIONS: Cast on 203 sts with Charcoal. K 6 rows. Work pattern Rows 3 & 4 for 12 rows. K 2 rows. K 2 rows with Celery, K 2 rows with Charcoal.
* With Celery, work pattern Rows 1 & 2 for 16 rows. K 2 rows.
  Olive, K 2 rows.
  Celery, K 2 rows.

With Olive, work pattern Rows 3 & 4 for 18 rows. K 2 rows.
  Celery, K 2 rows.
  Olive, K 2 rows.
With Celery, work pattern Rows 1 & 2 for 16 rows. K 2 rows.
  Charcoal, K 2 rows.
  Celery, K 2 rows.
With Charcoal, work pattern Rows 3 & 4 for 18 rows. K 2 rows.
  Celery, K 2 rows.
  Charcoal, K 2 rows.
Repeat directions from * twice more. Repeat again from * until 68 rows have been worked. With Charcoal, work pattern Rows 3 & 4 for 12 rows. K 6 rows and cast off. Block.

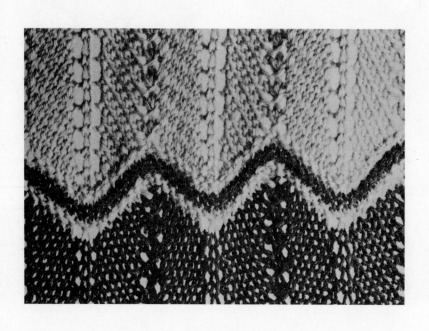

Bedspread knit in sections using lace and raised stitches, 19th century. Brooklyn Museum.

One section of bedspread. Four sections joined together to create pattern.

The garter stitch is used for the background.

potholders

BROWN AND BLUE POTHOLDER

this potholder is illustrated on page 64

SIZE: 8 inches square

MATERIALS: The American Thread Co., 70-yd. skeins
Aunt Lydia's Rug Yarn #215 Peacock 1 skein
Aunt Lydia's Rug Yarn #245 Brown 1 skein
Suggested needle size: no. 8; English no. 5
Crochet hook: size H (metal)

GAUGE: 4½ sts = 1 inch

PATTERN STITCH: Garter Stitch

DIRECTIONS: Cast on 35 sts with Brown. * K 1 with Brown, K 1 with Peacock, repeat from * across every row until piece measures 7½ inches. Cast off. With SC, crochet with Brown around four sides. Make a loop with 10 SC sts at one corner. Fasten to holder. Block.

KNITTING INTO ROW BELOW

Insert needle into stitch in row below as shown, and pull yarn through; then work next stitch as directed.

BRIGHT PINK POTHOLDER

this is shown on page 64

SIZE: 8¼ inches square

MATERIALS: The American Thread Co., 70-yd. skeins
Aunt Lydia's Heavy Rug Yarn Art. 235
#229 Watermelon 1 skein
Suggested needle size: no. 8; English no. 5
Crochet hook

GAUGE: 3½ sts = 1 inch

PATTERN STITCH: K 3, * K 1 into row below (see diagram to left), P 1, repeat from * across row, ending K 3.
Repeat this row for pattern stitch.

DIRECTIONS: Cast on 30 sts. K 6 rows. Work in pattern stitch for 56 rows. K 5 rows and cast off. Crochet a chain 4 inches long, and attach to potholder for loop. Block.

child's blanket

The yarn used here is variegated, combining yellow, orange, pink, and light pink in one strand. It is worked in the Cable Stitch. Use your leftover yarn to make a matching blanket for your child's doll's bed, or let your child knit one!

CHILD'S BLANKET

this blanket is shown on page 66

SIZE: 34 inches by 46 inches

MATERIALS: Coats & Clark, Inc., 3½-oz. skeins
4 ply knitting worsted #941
Summer Sunset 6 skeins
Suggested needle size: no. 9 circular;
English no. 4
Crochet hook: size H (metal)

GAUGE: 4 sts = 1 inch; 6 rows = 1 inch

PATTERN STITCH: Multiple of 12 plus 6. Combination of Garter, ribbing and Cable Stitches (see p. 29)
  Row 1, K 10, * K 6, P 6, repeat from * across row, ending K 16.
  Row 2, K 10, * P 6, K 6, repeat from * across row, ending P 6, K 10.
  Rows 3 and 5, repeat Row 1.
  Rows 4 and 6, repeat Row 2.
  Row 7, repeat Row 1, turning cable every K 6 rib.
  Rows 8, 10, and 12, repeat Row 2.
  Rows 9 and 11, repeat Row 1.
  Rows 13, 15, and 17, repeat Row 2.
  Rows 14, 16, and 18, repeat Row 1.
  Row 19, repeat Row 2, turning cable every K 6 rib.
  Rows 20, 22, and 24, repeat Row 1.
  Rows 21 and 23, repeat Row 2.
  Repeat these 24 rows for pattern.

DIRECTIONS: Cast on 134 sts. Work in Garter Stitch for 20 rows. Work 24 pattern rows 9 times. Work Pattern Rows 1-12. Work in Garter Stitch for 20 rows. Cast off. Block. Crochet 2 rows of SC across each end. Add fringe to four corners.

DOLL'S BLANKET

this blanket is shown on page 67

SIZE: 12 inches by 18 inches

MATERIALS: Coats & Clark, Inc., 3½-oz. skeins
4-ply knitting worsted #941
Summer Sunset 1 skein
Suggested needle size: no. 9; English no. 4
Crochet hook: size H (metal)

GAUGE: 4 sts = 1 inch

PATTERN STITCH: **Row 1,** * K 2, P 2, repeat from * across row, ending K 2.
  Row 2 * P 2, K 2, repeat from * across row, ending P 2.
  Row 3, repeat Row 2.
  Row 4, repeat Row 1.
  Repeat these 4 rows for pattern stitch.

DIRECTIONS: Cast on 50 sts and work in pattern stitch for 18 inches. Cast off. Crochet with SC across both ends. Block. Add fringe to four corners.

Detail of contemporary wool sock, Russian. Brooklyn Museum.

rugs

One neglected use for knitting is in making rugs. The ones shown are heavyweight and sturdy, knit with heavy rug yarn. As for all rugs, it is recommended that you use a pad under them. ■ The hot pink and orange rug is easy to make, a combination of Stockinette and Garter Stitches. ■ The K 1, Sl 1 technique makes a sturdy fabric suitable for rugs, as shown in the striped rug on opposite page. ■ The stair runner shown below is also suitable for hallways. With the directions given, it can be made to any desired length.

STRIPED RUG

this rug is shown on page 71

SIZE: 24 inches by 36 inches including edging

MATERIALS: Troy Yarn & Textile Co., 10-oz. skeins
Avanti 4 ply Rug Yarn #200   Orange   1 skein
Avanti 4 ply Rug Yarn #205   Nasturtium   1 skein
Avanti 4 ply Rug Yarn #400   Grass Green   1 skein
Avanti 4 ply Rug Yarn #505   Teal   1 skein
Avanti 4 ply Rug Yarn #909   Jet   1 skein
Suggested needle size: no. 8; English no. 5
Crochet hook: size J (metal)

GAUGE: 4 sts = 1 inch; 5½ rows = 1 inch

PATTERN STITCH: **Row 1,** * Sl 1 (keeping yarn to the back), K 1, repeat from * across row.
Row 2, * K 1, Sl 1 (bringing yarn to the front), repeat from * across row.
Row 3, * Sl 1 (bringing yarn to the front), K 1, repeat from * across row.
Row 4, * K 1, Sl 1 (keeping yarn to the back), repeat from * across row.

DIRECTIONS: Cast on 95 sts with Green.
Green: K 2 rows, work pattern Rows 1 & 2 for 28 rows;
*Jet: K 1 row, work Rows 3 & 4 & 3;
Nastu: K 1 row, work Rows 3 & 4 for 18 rows, work Row 3;

Jet: K 1 row, work Rows 2 & 1 & 2;
Teal: K 1 row, work Rows 2 & 1 in that order for 34 rows, work Row 2;
Jet: K 1 row, work Rows 3 & 4 & 3;
Orange: K 1 row, work Rows 3 & 4 for 18 rows, work Row 3;
*Jet: K 1 row, work Rows 2 & 1 & 2;
Green: K 1 row, work Rows 2 & 1 in that order for 26 rows, work Row 2;
Repeat directions from * to * once.
Green   K 1 row, work Rows 2 & 1 in that order for 28 rows, K 2 rows.
Cast off. Crochet 2 rows SC with Jet around all sides. Block.

STAIR RUNNER

this rug is shown on page 70

SIZE: 18 inches by 40 inches

MATERIALS: Troy Yarn & Textile Co.
Avanti 4 ply Rug Yarn   #105   Wine   10 oz.
Avanti 4 ply Rug Yarn   #108   Purple   10 oz.
Avanti 4 ply Rug Yarn   #300   Yellow   10 oz.
Avanti 4 ply Rug Yarn   #305   Olive   10 oz.
Suggested needle size: no. 10 circular; English no. 3

GAUGE: 4½ sts = 1 inch; 5 rows = 1 inch

PATTERN STITCH: Cross Stitch (see p. 29). Uneven number of sts.

Row 1, K 2, * skip one st, take needle behind it and K second st, leaving it on needle, K first st, Sl both sts off needle, repeat from * across row, ending K 1.

Row 2, P 2, * skip one st, P second st, leaving it on needle, P first st, Sl both sts off needle, repeat from * across row, ending P 1. Repeat these 2 rows for pattern stitch.

DIRECTIONS: Cast on 81 sts with Wine. K 1 row. Work Row 2 of pattern stitch.

  *Wine: work 2 rows of pattern stitch.
  Olive: work 2 rows of pattern stitch.
  Purple: work 2 rows of pattern stitch.
  Yellow: work 2 rows of pattern stitch.

Repeat these 8 rows four times more.

  Wine: work 4 rows of pattern stitch.
  Olive: work 4 rows of pattern stitch.
  Purple: work 4 rows of pattern stitch.
  Yellow: work 4 rows of pattern stitch.

Repeat these 16 rows once more.
Repeat directions from * once more.

  Wine: work 2 rows of pattern stitch.
  Olive: work 2 rows of pattern stitch.
  Purple: work 2 rows of pattern stitch.
  Yellow: work 2 rows of pattern stitch.

Repeat these 8 rows four times more.

  Wine: work Row 1 of pattern stitch.

Cast off tightly. Block.

PINK AND ORANGE RUG

this rug is shown on page 70

SIZE: 20 inches by 40 inches

MATERIALS: The American Thread Co., 70-yd. skeins
    Aunt Lydia's Heavy Rug Yarn Art 235
      #224 Bongo 9 skeins
    Aunt Lydia's Heavy Rug Yarn Art 235
      #227 Cerese 6 skeins
    Suggested needle size: no. 11
    Crochet hook: no. 10½ (wooden)

GAUGE: 2½ sts = 1 inch; 4 rows = 1 inch

PATTERN STITCH: 20 rows Stockinette Stitch alternate with 14 rows Garter Stitch

DIRECTIONS: Double strand of yarn used throughout. Cast on 70 sts with Bongo. * Work in Stockinette Stitch, 14 sts with Bongo, 14 sts with Cerese across row, for 20 rows. Work in Garter Stitch, 2 rows with Bongo, 2 rows with Cerese, for 14 rows. Work in Stockinette Stitch, 14 sts with Cerese, 14 sts with Bongo, across row, for 20 rows. Work in Garter Stitch, 2 rows with Cerese, 2 rows with Bongo, for 14 rows. Repeat from * once more. Work in Stockinette Stitch, 14 sts with Bongo, 14 sts with Cerese across row, for 20 rows. Cast off. With Cerese, crochet one row of SC around rug, being careful not to pull in edges. Work one row SC with Bongo. Block.

placemats

These mats are worked in variations of the Lace Stitch. Made of sturdy cotton or linen, they are very durable, belying their dainty appearance. To add body, dampen in starch before blocking after every washing. The lime and yellow mat can be made as long as desired, to serve as a table runner or a bureau scarf.

Pink and Orange Placemat—Lace Stitch

Lime and Yellow Table Runner—
Combining Stockinette and Lace Stitches

Blue and Green Placemat—Lace Stitch

placemats

RUST PLACEMAT

this placemat is shown on page 74

SIZE: 13 inches by 19 inches

MATERIALS: The Yarn Depot, Inc.
    10/2 linen   Rust   2½-oz. per mat
    Suggested needle size: no. 8; English no. 5
    Crochet hook: size F

GAUGE: 3½ sts = 1 inch

PATTERN STITCH: Lace Stitch. Multiple of 6 plus 12
  Row 1, K 7, * YO, P 2 tog, YO, P 2 tog, K 2, repeat from * across, ending K 7.
  Row 2, P 7, * YO, P 2, tog, YO, P 2 tog, P 2, repeat from * across, ending P 7.
  Repeat these 2 rows for pattern stitch.

DIRECTIONS: Yarn is used double throughout. Cast on 66 sts. Work in Stockinette Stitch for 8 rows. Work in pattern stitch for 42 rows. Work in Stockinette stitch for 7 rows and cast off. With SC, crochet around all sides of mat. Dampen in light starch and block.

PINK AND ORANGE PLACEMAT

this mat is shown on page 75

SIZE: 12½ inches by 18½ inches

MATERIALS: Coats & Clark, Inc.
Knit-Cro-Sheen Art. A 64 C
  #122 Watermelon 1 ball
Knit-Cro-Sheen Art. A 64 C
  #135c Tango 1 ball

Suggested needle size: no. 6; English no. 7
Crochet hook: size F

GAUGE: 5 sts = 1 inch (measure border sts)

PATTERN STITCH: Lace Stitch. Multiple of 12 plus 6
  Row 1, K 8, * K 2 tog, YO, K 2, YO, K 2 tog, P 6, repeat from * across row, ending K 8.
  Row 2, P 8, * P 6, K 6, repeat from * across row, ending P 14.
  Repeat these 2 rows for pattern stitch.

DIRECTIONS: Both yarns are knit together. Cast on 82 sts. Work in pattern stitch for 76 rows. Cast off. Using both yarns, crochet one row of SC around four sides of mat. Dampen with medium starch and block.

BLUE AND GREEN PLACEMAT

this is shown on page 75

SIZE: 12 inches by 18 inches

MATERIALS: The American Thread Co.
    Puritan   #13   Green   1 ball
    Puritan   #24   Turquoise   2 balls
    (2 balls Green & 4 balls Turquoise for 3 mats)
    Suggested needle size: no. 8; English no. 5
    Crochet hook

GAUGE: 3½ sts = 1 inch; 5 rows = 1 inch

PATTERN STITCH: Lace stitch. Multiple of 6 plus 8
  Row 1, K 4, * K 2 tog, YO, K 1, YO, K 2 tog, K 1, repeat from *, ending K 4.
  Row 2, P.
  Repeat these 2 rows for pattern stitch.

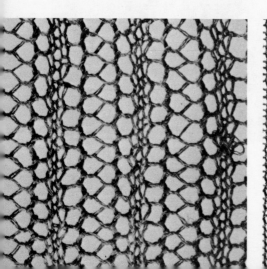
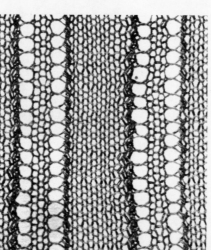
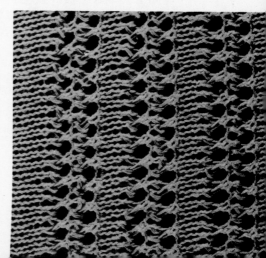

DIRECTIONS: Use three strands of yarn together throughout, two of Turquoise, one of Green. Cast on 67 sts. K 1 row and P 1 row. Work in pattern stitch for 52 rows. K 1 row. Cast off. Crochet one row of SC with three strands of yarn around four sides of mat. Dampen in medium starch and block.

LIME & YELLOW PLACEMAT (TABLE RUNNER)

this is shown on page 75

SIZE: 13 inches by 22 inches

MATERIALS: Diamond Yarn Corp., 50-gram balls
   Cote d'Azur Art 336 #185 Lime   1 ball
   Linor   Art 369 #47   Yellow 1 ball
   Suggested needle size: no. 4; English no. 9
   Crochet hook: size F

GAUGE: 4 sts = 1 inch; 4 rows = 1 inch (measure Lace Stitch)

PATTERN STITCH: Combination Stockinette and Lace Stitches
  Row 1, Lime: K.
  Row 2, Lime: P.
  Row 3, Yellow: K.
  Row 4, Yellow: P.
  Row 5, Lime: K 3, * YO, K 1, repeat from * across row, ending P 2.
  Row 6, Lime: P 2, * K 2 tog, repeat from * across row, ending P 2.
  Row 7, Yellow: K 2, * YO, K 2 tog, repeat from * across row, ending K 1.
  Row 8, Yellow: K.

DIRECTIONS: Cast on 55 sts with Lime. Work 8 pattern rows 3 times. * Work Rows 1 through 4. Work 8 pattern rows once. Work Rows 1 through 4. Work 8 pattern rows 3 times. Repeat from * once more. Work Rows 1 through 4. Cast off. With SC, crochet with Lime around four sides. Dip into medium starch and block.

Details, from left to right: the rust placemat, the pink and orange placemat, and the table runner.

WHITE AND GOLD PLACEMAT

this mat is shown above

SIZE: 12 inches by 18 inches

MATERIALS: Coats & Clark, Inc., 100-yd. balls
   Knit-Cro-Sheen Art 64M #1 White 3 balls
   Suggested needle size: no. 6; English no. 7
   Crochet hook: size F

GAUGE: 4 sts = 1 inch; 4 rows = 1 inch

PATTERN STITCH: Lace Stitch. Multiple of 4 plus 1
  Row 1, K 2, * YO, K 2 tog, K 2, repeat from * across row, ending K 1.
  Row 2, P.
  Row 3, K 4, * YO, K 2 tog, K 2, repeat from * across row, ending K 3.
  Row 4, P.
  Repeat these 4 rows for pattern stitch.

DIRECTIONS: Yarn is used double throughout. Cast on 69 sts and work in pattern stitch for 68 rows. Repeat Row 1 and cast off. With SC, crochet around 4 sides of mat. Dip in light starch and block.

Tote Bag, Hanger Covers and Greek Style Handbag

The simple Stockinette Stitch is used for the yellow, orange and khaki tote bag shown here. ■ Variegated yarn is used for the hanger covers. These are good gift items—easy and quick to knit. ■ Made with leftover rug yarn, the hot pink and red Greek-style handbag is a good project for imaginative use of color. Four-strand braid is used for the handles.

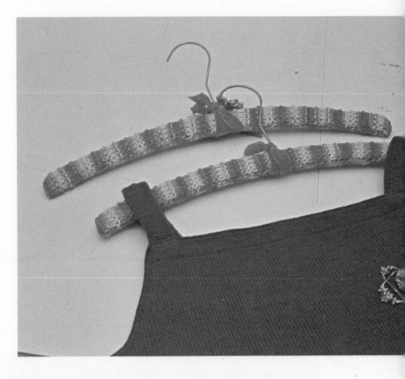

TOTE BAG

this bag is shown on page 78

SIZE: 16 inches square

MATERIALS: Paternayan Bros., Inc., 3-oz. skeins

Paterna Tapestry Knitting Yarn	#415	Yellow	1 skein
Paterna Tapestry Knitting Yarn	#417	Orange	1 skein
Paterna Tapestry Knitting Yarn	#911	Khaki	1 skein

Suggested needle size: no. 10; English no. 3
Crochet hook: size H

GAUGE: 3½ sts = 1 inch

PATTERN STITCH: Knit with yarn doubled in Stockinette Stitch, in the following color pattern:

Row 1, K 18 with Orange, K 18 with Khaki, K 18 with Yellow.
Row 2, P in color pattern of Row 1.
Row 3, repeat Row 1.
Row 4, repeat Row 2.
Row 5, K 15 with Orange, K 3 with Khaki, K 3 with Orange, K 12 with Khaki, K 3 with Yellow, K 3 with Khaki, K 15 with Yellow.
Row 6, P in color pattern of Row 5.
Row 7, repeat Row 5.
Row 8, repeat Row 6.

DIRECTIONS: Cast on 54 sts with Orange. Work 8 rows of pattern for 72 rows. Work Rows 1 & 2 for 72 rows. With Orange, K 1 row and cast off on P row. Block piece to 16 inches by 32 inches and fold in half. Sew sides together. Block. With SC, crochet with Orange around top edges. Handles: With Orange, crochet a chain of 60 sts and work 1 row of SC. With Yellow, work 1 row of SC around edges of handle. With Khaki, work one row of SC around edges of handle. Repeat directions for 2nd handle. Attach handles to bag. Line bag with gold felt.

Handbag and Kerchief Set

This kerchief may be worn pinned as shown, or tied under the chin with a ribbon. It is edged with black, matching the crochet handles of the bag. The Stockinette Stitch is used alone for the handbag, and in combination with the Garter Stitch for the kerchief. Try the two-color knitting technique described on p. 27 when knitting the handbag.

HANGER COVERS

these covers are shown on page 79

SIZE: 2½ inches wide

MATERIALS: Coats & Clark, Inc., 1-oz. skeins
    Red Heart Knitting Worsted   Art E 232
      #990   Roses   1 skein
    ⅝-inch velvet ribbon, 20 inches
    2 wooden coat hangers
    Suggested needle size: no. 6; English no. 7

GAUGE: 4 sts = 1 inch

PATTERN STITCH: Combination Stockinette and Garter Stitches

DIRECTIONS: Cast on 10 sts. Alternate 2 rows of Stockinette Stitch with 2 rows Garter Stitch for 116 rows. K 1 row, P 1 row. Cast off. With wrong side of cover facing out, sew cover together for half its length. Turn right side out, slip onto hanger and finish sewing together. Tie ribbon onto hanger.

NOTE: You may wish to give hanger a coat of gold paint.

HOT PINK AND RED BAG

this bag is shown on page 79

SIZE: 8 inches by 8½ inches

MATERIALS: Paterneyan Bros., Inc.
    Persian Rug Yarn   #242   Red   approx. 2½ oz.
    Persian Rug Yarn   #424   Orange   approx. 2½ oz.
    Persian Rug Yarn   #821   Cerese   approx. 2½ oz.
    Persian Rug Yarn   #827   Pink   approx. 2½ oz.
    Suggested needle size: no. 7; English no. 6
    Crochet hook: size F

GAUGE: 6 sts = 1 inch; 8 rows = 1 inch

PATTERN STITCH: Cross Stitch (see p. 29). Uneven number of sts
    Row 1, K 2 * skip one st. take needle behind it and K second st. leaving it on needle, K first st, Sl both sts off needle, repeat from * across row, ending K 1.
    Row 2, P.

Detail of the Hot Pink and Red Bag.

Row 3, K 1, * skip one st, take needle behind it and K second st, leaving it on needle, K first st, Sl both sts off needle, repeat from * across row, ending K 2.
Row 4, P.
Repeat these 4 rows for pattern stitch.

DIRECTIONS: Cast on 51 sts with Pink. K 1 row, P 1 row. Work even in pattern stitch, working 2 rows with Pink, 2 rows with Orange, 2 rows with Cerese and 2 rows with Red, until piece measures 15½ inches, ending with Row 1 of pattern stitch with Pink. Cast off tightly on P row. Block. Sew sides together and sew in a lining. With Pink, crochet with SC around top. Handle: with 4 strands of yarn, one of each color, make a braid 65 inches long. Make tassel at end by tying one strand around other three. Fasten handle to bag.

Detail of a 4-strand braid, using only 2 strands doubled. When using four separate strands, knot at top.

HANDBAG AND KERCHIEF

these are shown on page 81

SIZE: Adult

MATERIALS: Coats & Clark, Inc.
 4 ply Knitting Worsted Art. 234
   #943   Royal Court   1 skein
 4 ply Knitting Worsted Art. 234 #12   Black 1 skein
 Speed-Cro-Sheen   Art. C.44-C   Black 1 ball

 Suggested needle size: no. 5 (English no. 8) for
  Bag, no. 6 (English no. 7) for Kerchief
 Crochet hook: size F

GAUGE: **Bag:** 6 sts = 1 inch; **Kerchief:** 4 sts = 1 inch

PATTERN STITCH: Stockinette and Garter Stitches

DIRECTIONS: **Bag:** Cast on 58 sts on no. 5 needles with
Speed-Cro-Sheen.
Row 1, * K 2 with Royal Court, K 2 with Speed-Cro-
Sheen, repeat from * across row.
Row 2, * P 2 with Royal Court, P 2 with Speed-Cro-
Sheen, repeat from * across row.
Row 3, * K 2 with Speed-Cro-Sheen, K 2 with Royal
Court, repeat from * across row.
Row 4, * P 2 with Speed-Cro-Sheen, P 2 with Royal
Court, repeat from * across row.
Repeat these four rows 26 times more. Cast off with
Speed-Cro-Sheen. Block. With right sides facing,
sew sides together. Turn right side out and line with
black material. Handle: With black wool, crochet a
piece 43 inches long with 2 rows of SC and attach
ends to bag (see detail).

DIRECTIONS: **Kerchief:** Cast on 2 sts with Royal Court.
on no. 6 needles. **Row 1,** K 1, YO, K 1. **Row 2,** P. **Row 3,**
and all other *odd* rows, K 1, YO, K across, YO, K 1.
Rows 4, 10, 12, 18, 20, & 22, K. **Rows 6, 8, 14, 16, 24,
26, & 28,** P. Repeat these 28 rows twice more. K 10
rows and cast off. Crochet one row of SC around
edges with Black wool. Block.

Detail of Kerchief.

Handbag knit with metallic thread and silk, 19th century. This is a lovely example of stranded knitting. Freid-
man Collection, Brooklyn Museum.

hats, hooded scarf, and ski band

The blue and purple hat is a good project for introducing the beginner to four-needle (circular) knitting. It is worked in Ribbing and the Stockinette Stitch. ■ The red and white hat has an unusual pattern, a subtly curved shape to its design. The yarn used is very soft. ■ For the hooded scarf another variegated yarn was used, called Paisley Green. It is knit on the bias and is partially sewn along one side to form hood. ■ Another excellent project for leftover yarn, the ski band is easy and fast knitting. It is worked in Ribbing and the Garter Stitch.

BLUE STRIPED HAT

this hat is shown on page 84

SIZE: Adult

MATERIALS: Pauline Denham Yarns, Inc., 2-oz. skeins
Nomotta Actuella   #2301   Blue   1 skein
Nomotta Actuella   #2370   variegated 1 skein
Suggested needle size: dp (double pointed) no. 9;
English no. 4

GAUGE: 4 sts = 1 inch; 5 rows = 1 inch

PATTERN STITCH: Combination Ribbing and Stockinette Stitch

DIRECTIONS: Cast on 68 sts with variegated yarn. Divide onto 3 needles: 22 sts, 22 sts, 24 sts. Work in K 2, P 2 ribbing for 10 rows. Work even in ribbing pattern in the following color sequence: 1 row Blue, 1 row variegated yarn, 2 rows Blue, 2 rows variegated yarn, 3 rows Blue, 3 rows variegated yarn, 4 rows Blue, 4 rows variegated yarn. Divide sts to 23, 23, 22. * With variegated yarn, K 2 tog, k across needle; repeat for other 2 needles. K 1 row. Change to Blue and K 2 rows. Repeat from * until 3 sts remain. Cast off. Make tassel with variegated yarn.

RED AND WHITE HAT

this hat is shown on page 85

SIZE: Adult

MATERIALS: Columbia-Minerva Corp.
Featherweight   #650   Scarlet   1 ball
Reverie   #2319   Scarlet   1 ball
4 ply knitting worsted   White   1 oz.
Suggested needle size: dp no. 9; English no. 4

GAUGE: 4 sts = 1 inch; 5 rows = 1 inch

PATTERN STITCH: **Row 1,** Sl 1, K 1, PSSO, K across, ending YO, K 3; repeat for next 2 needles.
Row 2, P across row, P into *back* of YO sts; repeat for next 2 needles.
Row 3, Sl 1, K 1, PSSO, K to end; repeat for next 2 needles.
Row 4, K across row, K into *back* of YO sts; repeat for next 2 needles.

DIRECTIONS: Knit scarlets together and cast on 60 sts with them. Divide onto 3 needles.
Scarlet: Work pattern Rows 1 & 2 for 6 rows.
*White: Work Rows 1 & 2.
Scarlet: Work Rows 1 & 2.
Repeat from * for 24 more rows.

Scarlet: Work Rows 1 & 4 for 4 rows. Work Rows 3 & 4 for 10 rows.

White: Work Rows 3 & 2 in that order.

*Scarlet: Work Rows 3 & 2 in that order.

White: Work Rows 3 & 2 in that order.

Repeat from * for 4 more rows.

Scarlet: Work Rows 3 & 2 in that order for 18 rows. Cast off 3 sts remaining. Make tassel of white.

HOODED SCARF

this is shown on page 85

SIZE: 10 inches by 76 inches

MATERIALS: Pauline Denham Yarn Inc., 2-oz. skeins
Kensington #1228 Paisley Green 5 skeins
Suggested needle size: no. 15; English no. 000

GAUGE: 2½ sts = 1 inch

PATTERN STITCH: Bias Pattern
Row 1, K 1, YO, K across row, ending K 2 tog.
Row 2, K 7, P across row (P into back of YO st).
Repeat these 2 rows for pattern stitch.

DIRECTIONS: Cast on 25 sts. Work in pattern for 74 inches. Cast off. Block. Add fringe at both ends. Fold scarf in half, and sew two edges together to form back of hood—sew for 8 inches from fold.

SKI BAND

this is shown on page 85

SIZE: Adult

MATERIALS: Coats & Clark, Inc., 1-oz. skeins
4 ply knitting worsted Art E 232
#515 Dark Turquoise 1 skein
4 ply knitting worsted Art E 232
#676 Emerald 1 skein
Suggested needle size: no. 11

GAUGE: 3½ sts = 1 inch; 5 rows = 1 inch (measure Garter Stitch)

PATTERN STITCH: Combination Ribbing and Garter Stitch

DIRECTIONS: Both yarns are knit together. Cast on 12 sts. Work in K 1, P 1 ribbing for 7½ inches. Increase sts on next 4 rows: row 1, K 1, YO, K across row, ending YO, K 1; row 2, K across, K into *back* of YO sts; row 3, repeat row 1; row 4, repeat row 2. On 16 sts, work even in Garter Stitch for 11 inches. Decrease sts on next 3 rows: row 1, K 2 tog, K across row, ending K 2 tog; row 2, K across; row 3, repeat row 1. Cast off in K. Join ends. No blocking.

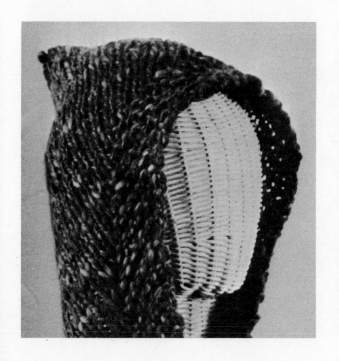

The items on these two pages and on pages 92-3 were designed and knit by villagers in Peru and Bolivia. Through an organization called PRODUCTS OF THE ALIANZA, crafts from Peru, Bolivia, Colombia, and Ecuador have been brought to the attention of North American merchants and distributors. This is a new program of self-help which has been developed in cooperation with the Alliance for Progress to assist South American artisans in organizing and operating cooperatives for the development, production, sale, and shipment of their unique products.

Colorful Peruvian handknit flowers made by villagers from the Puno area.

Knit toys such as these animals and boat with figures are typical examples of Peruvian handicraft.

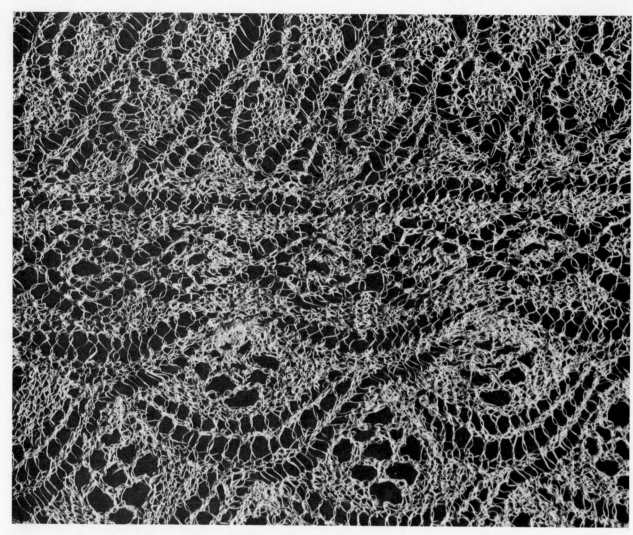

Detail of white mohair scarf using threadlike yarn. This scarf is similar to Shetland lace knitting. Brooklyn Museum.

french abbreviations

K	*point endroit*
P	*point envers*
ST (S)	*point(s)*
DEC(S)	*diminuez—diminutions*
INC(S)	*augmentez—augmentations*
TOG	*ensemble*
YO	*jeté*
PSSO	*passer point glissé*
SL	*glisser*
DP	*d'aiguilles*
CH	*chainette*
SC	*maille serrée*

* (SIGNE DE REPETITION) . . . . *suivez les instructions de * jusqu'au mot "répétez"; ensuite recommencez à **

german abbreviations

K	*rechts stricken*
P	*links stricken*
ST(S)	*masche(n)*
DEC(S)	*abnehmen*
INC(S)	*aufnehmen*
TOG	*zusammen*
YO	*umschlag*
PSSO	*die abgehobene Masche ueberziehen*
SL	*schlüpfen*
DP	*hilfsnadeln*
CH	*luftmasche(n)*
SC	*feste masche(n)*

* (STERN) . . . . . . *von * bis zum Wort wiederholen weiterarbeiten, dann beginne vom **

Detail of shawl, Pinta lace, knit with vegetable fiber. Made by nuns on the Island of Madeira. Brooklyn Museum.

spanish abbreviations

K . . . . *derecho*
P . . . . *reves*
ST(S) . . . . *puntada(s)*
DEC(S) . . . . *disminuir—disminuyendo*
INC(S) . . . . *aumentar—aumentando*
TOG . . . . *junto*
YO . . . . *hilo sobre la aguja*
PSSO . . . . *dejar pasar una puntada*
SL . . . . *pasar sin trabajando*
DP . . . . *punto doble*
CH . . . . *cadeneta*
SC . . . . *crochet sencillo*
* **(ASTERISCOS)** . . . *siga las instrucciónes desde el **
hasta la palabra repetida, entonces empezar desde el *

italian abbreviations

K . . . . *maglia—diritto*
P . . . . *rovescio*
ST(S) . . . . *punto*
DEC(S) . . . . *calatura—diminuire*
INC(S) . . . . *aumentare*
TOG . . . . *insieme*
YO . . . . *filo sopra il ferro*
PSSO . *fare l punto poi passarlo sopra quello che segue*
SL . . . . *passare o scivolare*
DP . . . . *doppio punto*
CH . . . . *catena*
SC . . . . *crochet*
* **(ASTERISCO)** . *seguire la direzione da * poi ripetere,*
dopo cominciare da tante volte quanto è indicato.

Knitted Bolivian pouch in bold colors with intricate pattern. It has four pockets and is worn tucked under the belt.

Peruvian wool shoulder bag. Of interest is its similarity to the Greek bag in style and design. A striking example of stranded knitting. From the author's collection.

Ski cap from Peru

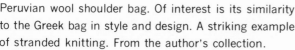

Nusta Virgin cap, worn by young girls in Peru to announce their availability for marriage. After the wedding the cap is hung on the wall for decoration.

Books

U.S.A.

BAXTER, Nancy, *Needlecraft for Home Decoration,* New York, Hearthside Press, 1966.

LANE, Rose Wilder, *American Needlework,* New York, Simon & Schuster for Woman's Day, 1963.

McCall's Treasury of Needlecraft, New York, Simon & Schuster for McCall's Corp., 1960.

EUROPEAN

DILLMONT, Thérèse de, *Encyclopedia of Needlework,* Mulhouse, France, D.M.C. Corp.

NORBURY, James, *Traditional Knitting Patterns,* London, Batsford, 1962.

NORBURY, James, AQUTTER, Margaret, *Odhams Encyclopedia of Knitting,* London, Odhams Press Ltd., 1957.

THOMAS, Mary, *Mary Thomas's Knitting Book,* London, Hodder and Stoughton Ltd., 1938.

THOMAS, Mary, *Mary Thomas's Book of Knitting Patterns,* London, Hodder and Stoughton Ltd., 1943.

PAPERBACKS

ABBEY, Barbara, *101 Ways To Improve Your Knitting,* New York, Viking Press, 1962.

O'MARA, Ruth Hatcher, *Easy Knitting,* New York, Pocket Books, 1965.

MAGAZINES

HANDWEAVER AND CRAFTSMAN, 246 Fifth Ave., New York, N.Y.

CRAFT HORIZONS, The American Craftsmen's Council, 16 East 52nd St., New York, N.Y.

BOOK SOURCES

THE YARN DEPOT, INC., 545 Sutter St., San Francisco, Cal.

CRAFT & HOBBY BOOK SERVICE, Dept. CH, Big Sur, Cal. 93920

MUSEUM BOOKS, INC., 48 E. 43rd St., N.Y., N.Y. 10017

JOAN TOGGITT, 52 Vanderbilt Ave., New York, N.Y.

Handknit wool ski band from South America with llama motif in white on black background.

SUPPLIERS

Listed here are the companies whose yarn was used for the projects in this book. If you are unable to obtain a particular yarn, write to the manufacturer to find out the store nearest you that carries it.

THE AMERICAN THREAD CO.
90 Park Ave.
New York, N.Y.

BEAR BRAND YARNS CO.
230 Fifth Ave.
New York, N.Y.

EMILE BERNAT & SONS CO.
P. O. Box 384
Uxbridge, Mass.

COATS & CLARK, INC.
430 Park Ave.
New York, N.Y.

COLUMBIA-MINERVA CORP.
15 E. 26th St.
New York, N.Y.

DIAMOND YARN CORP.
30 W. 26th St.
New York, N.Y. 10010

PATERNEYAN YARN CO.
312 E. 95th St.
New York, N.Y.

PAULINE DENHAM YARNS, INC.
Petaluma, Cal.

SPINNERIN YARN CO., INC.
230 Fifth Ave.
New York, N.Y.

TROY YARN & TEXTILE CO.
Pawtucket, R.I.

WILLIAM UNGER & CO., INC.
230 Fifth Ave.
New York, N.Y.

You may order yarn directly from:

THE YARN DEPOT, INC.
545 Sutter St.
San Francisco, Cal.

Detail of contemporary sock, Russian, using the crossed Easter stitch. Brooklyn Museum.

KNITTING NEEDLE COMPANIES:

SUSAN BATES—C. J. BATES & SON, INC.
Chester, Conn.

THE BOYE NEEDLE COMPANY
4335 N. Ravenswood Ave.
Chicago, Illinois

HERO MFG. CO. INC.
Middleboro, Mass.

If you wish more information about Alianza, you may write to:
PRODUCTS OF THE ALIANZA
7610 Empire State Building
New York, N.Y.

Antique evening purse, an example of fine bead knitting. In such a project
the design is carefully planned and the color beads threaded as required.